WALKING THE PATH

A Beginner's Guide to Spirituality

(*Simple Spiritual Journey Book 1*)

DE FLETCHER

Copyright © 2024 by De Fletcher. All rights reserved.

No portion of this book may be reproduced in any form without written permission from the publisher or author, except as permitted by US copyright law.

This publication is designed to provide accurate and authoritative information in regard to the subject matter covered. It is sold with the understanding that neither the author nor the publisher is engaged in rendering legal, investment, accounting or other professional services. While the publisher and author have used their best efforts in preparing this book, they make no representations or warranties with respect to the accuracy or completeness of the contents of this book and specifically disclaim any implied warranties of merchantability or fitness for a particular purpose. No warranty may be created or extended by sales representatives or written sales materials. Neither the publisher nor the author shall be liable for any loss of profit or any other commercial damages, including but not limited to special, incidental, consequential, personal, or other damages.

NO AI TRAINING: Without in any way limiting the author's [and publisher's] exclusive rights under copyright, any use of this publication to "train" generative artificial intelligence (AI) technologies to generate text is expressly prohibited. The author reserves all rights to license uses of this work for generative AI training and development of machine learning language models.

Paperback ISBN: 978-1-7379507-9-0

Published by Spirit Oaks Press

Book Cover Design by 100 Covers

First edition 2024

To my brother Don . . . I cannot thank you enough for supporting my journey.

So often our beliefs do not belong to us, but are things we accepted as truth and adopted from our teachers and experiences.

So often our beliefs align with neither our purpose nor our Highest Good.

So often we suffer needlessly, desperately holding onto the very things we should set free.

– De Fletcher

Contents

Preface		*i*
1	Do We Have Spiritual Abilities?	1
2	What Spiritual Abilities Do We Have?	5
3	Our Built-In Spiritual Knowledge	29
4	Our Learned Knowledge	49
5	The Power of Our Subconscious Mind	61
6	It Matters What We Think, Say, and Do!	71
7	Truths We Were Never Taught	79
8	What Do You Believe?	101
9	Changing Old Beliefs	119
10	Releasing Grief, Stress, Anger, and More (Healing Practices)	147
11	Living a Spiritual Life	171
12	Conclusion	185
BONUS: Staying Calm in a World Gone Slightly Mad		*189*
When is the Last Time You Had a Good Night's Sleep?		*197*

Contents (2)

About the Author	199
Coming Soon!	201
Also By De Fletcher	203
Acknowledgements	205

Preface

As a child, I knew things beyond my years. I could sense things others didn't, and hear whispers guiding me to know right from wrong. When I witnessed or experienced violence, abuse, prejudice, or racism, it hurt my soul. It felt as if I came from a world of higher wisdom, peace, and harmony among all.

Like most children, my early training and experiences forced my inherent knowing into silence. The silencing didn't happen overnight, but came about slowly. So slowly, I didn't even realize when my guiding voice went silent. My inner guidance would briefly emerge over the years, then fall back into silence. Clearness came during moments of danger or despair. I realized then the help I'd received as a child hadn't gone away. There it remained, ready for me to rediscover it.

In my early thirties, I had what I call my "crazy, white girl, mental breakdown". I was doing my best to use what I was taught and believed would bring me happiness and prosperity, but it wasn't working. My life was like playing the song *Crazy Train* on repeat. I was miserable. I decided on a fresh approach to living and reconnecting with my inner guidance.

Since that day, I've spent years learning and practicing how to wake up my spiritual abilities. Certain lessons were unnecessarily complex or time-consuming.

It was during those times I realized the essence of spirituality is simplicity. So, I used my ability to simplify concepts and practices to teach others what I had learned. I'm now sharing my discoveries through the *Simple Spiritual Journey* series so others won't have to spend years (like I did) learning the basics.

The *Simple Spiritual Journey* series is structured as a daily spiritual way of living. I've done my best to create a resource for people of various beliefs to utilize. If you see a term that doesn't sit well with you, exchange it for one you prefer. In this way, you can use the terms you're comfortable with. Using terms you are familiar with (from your belief perspective) will assist you in learning on a whole new level.

This book is based upon the information and practices I've learned while walking my spiritual path for over twenty years. It includes information I've received from spiritual communications, things I've learned from classes, and experiences I've had while on my journey. Each chapter contains spiritual concepts, examples, and exercises to help reinforce what you're learning. The concepts and practices are simple and easy to understand. They are designed to assist you in opening yourself to new possibilities.

The information is presented as if we are in class together. My writing style may seem a little strange at first, but it will help you relate better to me and the material.

To get the most immediate and powerful results, set your intention to be open to experience each chapter and practice. As you read each chapter, take notes and complete the practices as you go. <u>I highly recommend buying a journal and writing in it every day</u>. Journal any thoughts, answers to questions, and experiences you have as you make your way through the book. Writing by hand reinforces what you are learning and experiencing. Returning to your writings later will help you see your progress and better understand yourself.

The number one rule is take your time! There's no reason to hurry, so work at your own pace. Don't let fear hold you back from learning and growing! Unlike school or college where knowledge is gained through book learning, spiritual knowledge is gained through practical experience. In other words, we have to experience and practice our spiritual abilities. Only by using them can we become comfortable and make them a part of us. Once you become comfortable with the information and practices, make them your own by using terms from your belief system. Then create a daily routine that assists you in creating a less stressful life with more balance and happiness.

My purpose in writing this book is to provide you with easy-to-understand concepts and practices that nourish your soul. If you're just starting out, great! If you've been dabbling for a bit, super!

I believe anyone can learn something (even if it's just a new perspective) from experiencing this book. You have everything you need to get started. If you didn't, you wouldn't be here. You wouldn't be asking the questions or wanting answers if you were not ready! Have faith in your own timing to uncover your true power! <u>You are not alone</u> on this journey.

The *Simple Spiritual Journey* series is a self-study school covering the basics and beyond. It's for people who want to:

- Explore their own unique abilities or dive deeper into strengthening them.
- Change their life by choosing a different way of doing things.
- Create their own ceremonies, traditions, or rituals.
- Seek balance from trusting the guidance they receive from their Divine Self and Source.

This book is not designed as a substitute for professional heath care. **Please consult your primary care physician or mental health practitioner before making any changes to your diet, exercise, or daily mental health guidelines given to you by your healthcare team!**

If the way you were taught to live to find joy and success isn't working, and you want a long-lasting solution, you've arrived at the perfect destination! With that said, I'm excited to begin this journey with you! Let's get started with some basic spiritual truths . . .

1
Do We Have Spiritual Abilities?

The eyes of the people were opened, and those who chose to see recognized The Truth before them.

Have you ever visited a psychic or medium and wondered how they knew stuff about you? What did you think when they revealed past, present, or future information to you? How did you feel receiving messages from your loved ones? After your session, did you think the psychic or medium was special somehow? If you've never experienced a psychic or medium, have you watched or read stories about people who assisted police in solving crimes using their special abilities? What thoughts crossed your mind as the story unfolded? Did these stories make you believe that only some individuals can possess knowledge beyond normal senses?

It's possible you've been taught to distrust those who claim to possess these talents. Perhaps you believe what they are practicing goes against the teachings of *The Holy Bible* or other religious texts. People with such beliefs typically avoid psychic readings and medium visits. They do not follow stories about people who help police solve murders, find missing people, or identify human remains. They strongly oppose such activities.

Reflect on your personal experiences for a moment. Have you ever had a gut feeling or intuition that made you change your plans? Has a place felt familiar, despite you never visiting it before? Have you been in the middle of a conversation and felt like you had the same conversation before? Maybe you got a bad feeling about someone you just met. Perhaps you experienced something different (seeing dead people or dreaming of an event before it happened). If you've experienced any, what were your thoughts at that time? Were you afraid? Was your head filled with negative thoughts about your state of mind? Did your brain go into overdrive trying to rationalize what happened? Perhaps you thought you could have gifts as well.

Having these experiences doesn't make you crazy. You're not losing your mind. Everyone has these experiences (yes, everyone)! We may brush them off or deny their existence because we don't understand them.

Maybe our parents, extended family, peers, or religious leaders did not believe in these abilities, so we were taught not to believe in them. Perhaps we had something happen that really terrified us, and we're reluctant to experience it again. Just because we do not believe we have spiritual gifts doesn't mean we don't have them.

Some believe gifted psychics, mediums, or healers possess abilities beyond ordinary reach. The people we consider gifted simply acknowledged and nourished their particular abilities. They tended a spiritual garden whose seeds lay dormant, watered those seeds over time, and experienced them grow to their full potential.

You are not alone if the possibility of having spiritual gifts crossed your mind, but you dismissed them. If you believe you are not a "chosen" one, many people feel this way. The beliefs we have about our spiritual abilities may be the very things preventing us from discovering our own unique gifts! We will discuss beliefs further in a later chapter. For now, let's briefly talk about truth.

What is "a truth"? A truth is constant and never changes. It remains after all the things we believe to be true fall away. Our true nature is a spiritual being experiencing a physical life. Our creator made us perfect beings, with the ability to be good, loving, helpful, heal ourselves and others, and live a happy, prosperous life. We were born with a body, mind, and spirit.

Each of us is a spiritual being, housed within a physical body, living a human experience on Earth. It is who and what we are.

<u>We were all born with what I call a Spiritual Operating System (OS)</u>. This system is our **inherent knowledge**. Part of our Spiritual OS is the spiritual gifts. Simply put, gifts are not exclusive to the special or chosen ones. They are built in! We **all** have them and can choose whether or not we want to use them (Free Will). (We will do a deep dive on our Spiritual OS in the third chapter.)

We are also born with the ability to gain knowledge through training and experiences. This is called **learned knowledge**. Our inherent knowledge, learned knowledge, and subconscious mind all work together to create the life we are experiencing. They are all working in the background, and it is our words, thoughts, feelings, and actions guiding them!

To understand how these four systems rely on each other to create our experience, we'll explore each in the following chapters. Let's begin with the spiritual gifts we all came here with!

2
What Spiritual Abilities Do We Have?

We are SO much more than we have been led to believe!

Many people believe the spiritual gifts we have work independently of our five human senses. The term ESP (Extra-Sensory Perception) is used to describe the use of our spiritual abilities. The definition of ESP varies, depending on the source. Most sources agree with it coming from something other than the known senses. The *New Oxford American Dictionary* defines ESP as "The faculty of perceiving things by means other than the known senses." It's even referred to as a "sixth sense".

These definitions seem to be based on a belief that a person must have a sixth sense. It also seems to invoke the unexplained by using the words "other than the known". Maybe these definitions aim to mystify these abilities.

Wikipedia defines spiritual terms using the word "claimed" despite many proven instances of spiritual abilities in people. Could it be these gifts are simply an extension of our known senses?

In my experience, the spiritual abilities we all have come from our five senses and are part of our inherent knowledge. We either use them in a spiritual or physical way, depending on the source of the input. If we indeed have a sixth sense, it would be the gift of "knowing". Even this gift uses the other five senses to gather information quickly, compile the data, and determine an answer to various situations.

Remember, we are body, mind, and spirit. Each of these have their own knowledge set. For example, our body (physical knowledge) knows to breathe and sustain a heartbeat automatically. Why would we choose to believe our spiritual knowledge is incapable of the same type of inherent inner workings? Perhaps it's because many of us were never taught to access our spiritual side.

We are all spiritual beings with a direct connection to All That Is (Spirit, God, Creator, Universe). We don't require intermediaries or something outside ourselves to connect with our spiritual abilities or communicate with Source. These tools are built-in! People may view spiritual gifts as not real, only for special people, or somehow spooky or evil, because society has presented and taught them in those ways for millennia.

WHAT SPIRITUAL ABILITIES DO WE HAVE?

Have you ever watched a paranormal-type show on TV and paid attention to the music, sound effects, or visual effects used? Often they create a mysterious (and sometimes scary) type of reaction from the audience! TV stands for television. When we say the word, it sounds like "tell-a-vision," does it not? The shows we watch on TV are called "programs". Just something to think about.

As discussed earlier, many people will question whether they have spiritual gifts. Others believe that only "special" people receive spiritual abilities. Some individuals may believe the teachings they received growing up forbid using these type of abilities. Others tremble at the mere thought of anything spiritual because they've had frightening experiences in the past. Again, these beliefs are <u>based upon our training and experiences</u> (learned knowledge) and conflict with universal laws or spiritual truths. It's not about which beliefs are right or wrong, but which beliefs bring a balanced, happy life through honoring your spiritual knowledge and abilities.

It doesn't have to take a long time to erase doubts we have about our spiritual gifts. Our false beliefs (learned knowledge) serve as a roadblock to our spiritual progress. For example, a person believes only "gifted" people have spiritual abilities. They are trying to learn about their gifts, but it's slow-going. This person is experiencing cognitive dissonance (a contradiction between what they believe and what they want to believe).

So, how did we get to the point where we only experience brief glimpses of our inherent spiritual abilities? It's the imbalance between our inherent knowledge, learned knowledge, and what we focus our energy on each day (through what we think, say, and do). It's also about how print, audio, video, and in-person presentations shape our understanding of spiritual concepts. We learned to believe certain things about our spiritual side. Our prominent information sources then reinforce these learned beliefs.

Let's say a person wants to learn more about their spiritual gifts. Their inherent spiritual knowledge is prompting them to explore their spiritual side. Similar to the example, they believe only specific individuals possess spiritual abilities. The teachings and experiences they had led them to believe they were not special or gifted, affecting their self-worth. They reinforce their self-worth through daily thoughts, words, and actions. The subconscious uses those "unworthy" thoughts, words, emotions, and actions to ensure that person receives what they've focused their energy on that day (and every day).

So, the negative cycle and doubt sabotage their efforts to discover a whole new world of their spiritual self. This is why some things never seem to change in life, even though we would love for them to!

How do we fix the imbalance between learned and spiritual knowledge? We change any beliefs (and release any negatives) that no longer serve our Highest Good first! Don't spend years making slow progress (like I did) because of the beliefs and behaviors blocking your path. Instead, identify the beliefs that need changing based on spiritual truths. Choose to let go of the past (learn from it, forgive yourself and others, heal, then leave it in the past).

The beliefs we have result from what we learned (and agreed to) at an early age. They may not align with spiritual truth. The influence the past has on our life will remain until we learn how to let it go. We may feel a need to hang onto it. Sometimes the pain (or anger) we feel about the past is the only control we believe we have over those experiences.

The only difference between you and someone who uses their spiritual abilities well is they have had more practice. It's not that you weren't worthy of getting them! As we explore the specific spiritual gifts (and how we can use them), remember that nothing is broken or defective in terms of your spiritual abilities! We only need to wake them from "sleep mode" (like we do a computer after it hasn't been used for a while). Every person has all the spiritual abilities. One or two may be stronger when you first start out. We will cover how to discover your gifts and begin practicing them in another book in this series.

Types of Spiritual Gifts

I enjoy keeping things simple, so the easiest way to explain the spiritual gifts is: Using the physical senses in spiritual ways. This means using your five senses to pick up even more information. People were mostly taught to use their senses in the normal, physical way. Frankly, the term "normal" is very subjective. Had we been taught to use our spiritual gifts as children, we would believe <u>not</u> using them to be abnormal!

So, when we use our senses spiritually, we are able to sense the more subtle things in everyday life. Seeing a person in the middle of the road (who isn't there) is an example of using our sense of sight in a spiritual way. In this example, the eyes pick up on a spirit or residual energy (spirits and energy have different vibrational frequencies than a physical person). When we use our spiritual sight, we pick up on these energies and vibrational frequencies.

Spiritual Gifts Defined

The spiritual gifts are called "Clair____". Clair means clear. It comes from the Latin word "Clarus," which means "clear, bright, or distinct". Clair is combined with words that describe one or more of the senses mentioned in the previous paragraphs.

Although the terms and definitions vary somewhat between spiritual beliefs and practitioners, all clairs are related to one or more of the five senses. There are a variety of clairs, depending on the source used to define them. To keep things simple, I'll cover seven here:

1. Claircognizance-clear knowing.
2. Clairvoyance-clear seeing.
3. Clairaudience-clear hearing.
4. Clairsentience-clear feeling.
5. Clairalience-clear smelling.
6. Clairgustance-clear tasting.
7. Clairtangency-clear touch.

Some Ways Spiritual Gifts Are Used

As mentioned previously, we were all born with **all** the spiritual gifts. It's been my experience that one or two will be stronger than the others when we first reawaken them. The more you practice your spiritual abilities, the stronger they become. Your weaker abilities will also strengthen. For example, when I first started exploring my gifts, I would hear and know things. As I used these in my spiritual work, other abilities started showing up. I saw video clips (like TikTok videos) in my mind's eye, smelled perfume and smoke, felt what others were feeling, and more.

Below are descriptions of the spiritual abilities and some ways you can use them.

Clear Knowing

A person with clear knowing just knows things. If you ask, they won't be able to tell you how they know, just that they do. They have filtered all the surrounding stimuli (and translated it into what's going on) without any conscious thought. This includes data from inside and outside themselves. They filter all this data so fast they don't even realize they're doing it.

An example would be a detective trying to solve a homicide case. The detective brings in a person for questioning. The person doesn't say or do anything to raise suspicion, but the detective "knows" this person is the one they're looking for. Turns out, the person has an alibi and the police have nothing to hold him on, so they have to release him. Once the investigation is complete, the evidence leads right back to the person the detective "knew" was the perpetrator!

Clear Seeing

A person has clear vision when they see information about a person, object, location, scenario, or event through their mind's eye.

They may have prophetic dreams or see things others don't notice (like small details or spirits). They may also see writing, pictures, or symbols that aren't there. Their eyes filter and translate everything they see into what was, is, or will be.

An example would be a person whose dreams come true (foretelling), who sees replays of past events (like crimes), sees a person's true personality beneath their public facade, and much more.

Clear Hearing

A person with clear-hearing can hear things most people don't. They hear sounds in ranges outside normal human hearing. They may also hear spirits, animals, or what someone is saying versus the words coming out of their mouth. Perhaps they hear in other languages as well.

For example, a clear-hearing person is at a party having a conversation with someone. The clear-hearing person will hear what the other person is saying and receive a "translation" of it. So, clear hearing can discern lies, deception, emotions, state of mind, and much more.

Clear Feeling

A person with clear-feeling feels the vibration or emotions of people, the environment, situations, spirits, and more. They may take on the emotions of others.

For example, a clear-feeling person is listening to a friend talking about the summer heatwave. She can feel her friend's sadness, even though the friend never mentions feeling that way. A person with this gift may also become sad.

Clear Smelling

A person with clear-smell can smell aromas not present. Their sense of smell is highly developed and they smell things others do not.

An example would be a person who offers readings as a psychic or medium. During a reading, they tell you they are picking up a smell and describe it to you. You recognize it as your deceased mother's favorite flower.

Clear Tasting

A person with clear taste can taste something related to a person, event, environment, and more. They know what the taste is, even if they've never tasted it before.

An example would be a medium reading for a person wanting to connect with deceased loved ones. The medium may describe a woman and the taste of cherry pie. The person knows from this information the deceased relative is their aunt who loved cherry pie.

Clear Touching

A person with clear touch can touch personal items, objects, people, and more and receive information. This is called psychometry. They may get bits of information from what they touch, or they may receive a "download" of events, history, and more.

For example, some psychics help police solve missing persons or homicide cases by touching a photograph or personal item. They receive information from the item, then relay that information to the police. Received information may include the person's status, location, involved individuals, and much more.

Using Your Abilities

Everyone is born with all the gifts, but each person is different in which gifts they use and how they use them. As they discover their gifts, they develop their own way of receiving spiritual information through their gifts and spiritual connection.

So, we custom design our way of doing things! You may have heard the phrase, "There are many paths." This is so true! Each person creates "their way" as they learn about spirituality. Just as you will learn the practices in this book and change them to best suit your life!

Everyone chooses how and **if** they want to use their spiritual abilities. We may use them to become a better parent, protect the Earth, help our children, reduce stress and drama, be a better friend, love yourself, or be a healer for others. The choices are as unique and limitless as DNA!

My Experiences

The first spiritual gift I recognized (one of my strongest) was knowing. As I mentioned earlier, I just knew things as a child. I couldn't explain how I knew not to go down a certain street or trust a certain person. It was almost like having a built-in lie detector, radar/sonar, and guidance system. Of course I didn't know what it was at the time. I just trusted and used it naturally. In retrospect, I believe I was using my inherent spiritual abilities before they were silenced by my training.

Since I started reawakening my spiritual abilities (over twenty years ago), I've had experiences most people would not believe.

WHAT SPIRITUAL ABILITIES DO WE HAVE?

I've seen a mountain cry, talked to Archangel Azrael before a loved one passed, heard birthday greetings from deceased relatives, and saw my ancestors lining up at The Doorway to greet a relative as they were crossing over.

Other experiences include watching a mini video of a man's childhood past, seeing a group of Native Americans traveling through the fog, and witnessing a dark, stormy day turn into blue skies and sun as a relative was buried. The last ten-plus years have provided enough experiences to fill an entire book. Perhaps (in the future), I'll write a book about all my experiences, but for now, I'd like to share an experience I had when several of my spiritual gifts converged while watching a movie . . .

The Book of Eli **Experience**

I was watching the movie *The Book of Eli* for the second or third time. There's a street scene where the main character (played by Denzel Washington) is confronted by a post-apocalyptic warlord (played by Gary Oldman). The warlord is looking for "The Book". Early on, the audience isn't told what book he's looking for, but they are shown he'll threaten, bribe, kidnap, or kill for this book. The warlords' mercenaries are on a mission to find this book. It's apparent they've been searching for this book for quite some time.

The scene was tense when I'd watched it before, but nothing out of the ordinary happened to me while viewing it. This time, I felt the need to pay close attention to it. The scene started, and I felt time slow down. I became fixated on this one scene and wasn't able to continue with the rest of the movie. The only way for me to move past it was to watch the scene multiple times and write the entire dialogue between the two characters!

Once that was done, I starting reviewing my notes on the dialogue. While reading those, the deeper message from that scene came into my awareness. I instantly understood why I felt compelled to watch the scene and record everything the characters said! Then, as if on cue, time returned to normal.

I've shared what came to me from translating that scene below. Approach it with an open mind and contemplate the supporting evidence. . .

The Book of Eli (Street Scene)

A secret war has been ongoing over *The Holy Bible*. The power of what's in it. This secret war is one of good versus evil, freedom versus slavery, or light versus dark. *The Holy Bible* (original version) has the power to help the people understand who/what they are, why they are here, and what they can do (if they so choose).

Those in power withhold this knowledge from the masses (and have been doing so for millennia). They hide **The Truth** from the masses by subverting it in their translations and teachings. By doing this, they maintain control over the people!

In earlier times, the priests would give their sermons in Latin. The majority didn't speak this language. The people who held power over them often forced people to follow a certain religion (even abandon their own religion). Those in power compelled them to obey religious edicts and prescribed behaviors upon threat of death. Those in power did their best to demoralize the people and destroy any trace of their true origins.

Over time, these compromised teachings subverted the original teachings of various religious texts (not just *The Holy Bible*). The Truth was "translated" to teach people a modified version of the original stories and teachings. Corruption in the churches, sexual deviancy by priests, and crimes/wars in the name of religion became commonplace. Concealing The Truth endured for millennia, but lies are always brought to the light. Hiding their deeds in plain sight was no longer working to enslave the people.

The people started waking from their slumber of spirit. They no longer tolerated the negative in their world and living under oppression. People demanded freedom to be themselves.

After the chaos, a powerful awakening occurred as The Light triumphed over darkness. It was a new beginning. Peace reigned as love and light triumphed over darkness for a thousand years. (A glimpse of the past, present, and future.)

Examples:

The Holy Bible serves as a how-to guide, addressing our identity, purpose, and spiritual abilities. It also provides a road map of the best ways to live our lives with less stress, drama, trauma, and grief. If you feel a disconnect between what you learned in church services and what is written in the Bible, you are right.

This religious text was translated from its original language, and those in power altered various passages to keep the masses unaware of The Truth. The warlord from *The Book of Eli* knew the true power of the book. He wanted to wield that power himself. It's why he would stop at nothing to get a copy of that book!

Again, this was revealed to me during a spiritual experience. It is a prime example of inherent knowledge being transmitted or "remembered"! You decide what you want to believe about it. While writing about this experience, some Bible verses came to mind. They are examples of this religious text's power to awaken and reveal our capabilities.

WHAT SPIRITUAL ABILITIES DO WE HAVE?

Remember, we always receive our spiritual communication from our own point of view. I experienced Christian churches growing up, so this is the reason these particular verses came to me. When we are open to our inherent knowledge, it will come to us in our own belief system and experiences. Contemplate what you were taught to believe about these verses or topics as you read each of them. Write your thoughts in your journal.

John 14:12 (KJV)

"Verily, verily, I say unto you, He that believeth in me, the works that I do shall he do also; and greater *works* than these shall he do; because I go unto my Father."

This verse lets us know we can also do the "works" Jesus did (miracles, healing, etc.). We just have to believe we have the "spark of God" ("unto my Father") within us and remember how to use it. That's what Jesus did. He used the spark of God (Source/Creation) within him to do His works.

Matthew 18:3 (KJV)

"And said, Verily I say unto you, except ye be converted, and become as little children, ye shall not enter into the kingdom of heaven."

Converted is to believe and trust in God/Source/Universe (or that you're a spiritual being). How we "become as little children" again is to return to our original programming (what we came here with). What we came here with is our inherent spiritual knowledge (Source OS)!

Luke 17:21 (KJV)

"Neither shall they say, lo here! or, lo there! for, behold, the kingdom of God is within you."

We cannot find Source or All That Is by searching outside ourselves. Our spiritual self (and all the gifts and knowledge) isn't "out there" somewhere. It lives within us. It is our spirit (soul) and our connection to Source.

Matthew 7:7–8 (KJV)

"Ask, and it shall be given you; seek, and ye shall find; knock, and it shall be opened unto you: For every one that asketh, receiveth; and he that seeketh, findeth; and to him that knocketh it shall be opened."

This is all about asking for help, setting your intent, and taking action to realize your goals, dreams, and spiritual abilities. It reminds us we have help. Just ask and doors will open! This applies to everyone, not just to those we believe are chosen or gifted. **We are all chosen and gifted!**

WHAT SPIRITUAL ABILITIES DO WE HAVE?

One religious teaching I remember from childhood is we aren't able to talk directly to God or Jesus. We must do it through a religious leader or our husband (depending on the religion). Some churches I attended taught <u>their religion was the only right one</u>, dictated the clothing a member must wear, or how they must keep their hair. Why would religion be concerned about what a person wears or their hairstyle versus saving a person's soul or assisting in their spiritual growth? The answer came into clear focus after my experience with that one scene from *The Book of Eli*.

Practice: Waking Your Spiritual Gifts

The less we use our inherent abilities, the more they stay in a kind of sleep mode. They wake up when needed, but mostly "snooze" because they're not being used. To awaken our spiritual gifts, we simply need to set our intent. Like when we wake from sleeping, our gifts will be a little groggy at first. Just like us, they require time and engagement to be fully awake.

<u>This practice is designed to help you</u>:
Wake your unique spiritual gifts, be open to using them, and receiving guidance from your Divine Self and Source.

<u>When you can do this practice</u>:
You only have to do this practice once!

<u>Time needed</u>: 5 minutes.

<u>What you will need</u>:

1. A quiet, comfortable, space.
2. Something comfortable to sit or lay on.
3. Your journal and something to write with.

<u>Reminder</u>:
Review the entire practice (including the notes) before completing this practice. Write about your experience in your journal.

<u>Follow these steps</u>:

1. Sit or lay in a comfortable position.
2. **Breathe in.** Through your nose, slowly filling your belly with air.
3. **Breathe out.** Through your mouth (slow and easy) until your belly goes flat.
4. **Continue deep breathing.** For a few minutes until you feel relaxed.

WHAT SPIRITUAL ABILITIES DO WE HAVE?

5. **Breathe out and say:** "I am waking my spiritual gifts and trusting my Highest Self and Source."
6. **Breathe in and say:** "I am."
7. **Breathe out and visualize:** Your body and mind releasing any tension or stress and completely relaxing.
8. **Breathe in and visualize:** White light coming into your body.
9. **Continue deep breathing.** Continue to focus on breathing and filling your body with white light until you feel you're finished.

NOTE 1: You may see, hear, or feel images, colors, or sensations coming from your chest, stomach, or other areas. Don't worry about getting overwhelmed! You won't get more than you're ready to receive right now. It's just how it works.

NOTE 2: Using "I AM." in the exercises is using the name of Spirit (God, Universe, Creation) to create. It also implies that whatever you are creating is already done (right now versus in the future)!

NOTE 3: Each person will have their own unique experience (each person receives what they need).

You may have a lot happen, nothing at all, or something in-between. The activation works **in your time** and **in the best way for you.**

NOTE 4: If you feel anxious, focus on your breathing! Feel the air flowing into your nose, your belly filling with air, and the air leaving your body through your mouth as your belly goes flat.

NOTE 5: As you remember your gifts and begin receiving guidance, you may feel a little strange. You are using your abilities more and they feel different from the logical brain you are used to using. You're beginning to make life better and you're feeling it. Things won't continue as they have in the past. You are growing!

NOTE 6: You will also experience increased energy, feel happier or lighter, and more creative! Treat yourself well. Get plenty of rest. Eat high-quality food and drink plenty of spring or filtered water (avoid tap water or "drinking" water).

NOTE 7: Recommend doing this practice outside in nature!

WHAT SPIRITUAL ABILITIES DO WE HAVE?

In this chapter, we've talked about what spiritual gifts are and how they are used. We also discovered each person uses their gifts in ways unique to them. We understand how false beliefs are a block to reawakening our spiritual abilities. False beliefs are like the weeds that pop up on your lawn. You can mow over them, but soon they're back, ruining the beauty of your lawn. We remove weeds by removing their roots. The roots that need to be removed to realize our spiritual beauty are our false beliefs.

In the next chapter, we will take a deep dive into our powerful inherent knowledge. I refer to it as our Source OS (Operating System).

3
Our Built-In Spiritual Knowledge

So often we spend a lifetime searching outside ourselves for the very things that reside Within.

In the last two chapters, we discussed types of spiritual gifts and how we are **all** born with them as part of our inherent knowledge package. Now we will explore what this package is, what it contains, and how it works with our learned knowledge and subconscious mind to create our life experiences.

Our inherent knowledge package is what I call our Source OS (Operating System). This Source OS is our "spiritual source code" and contains a database of all spiritual information, skills, and abilities. It is how we are hard-wired. Much like our bodily functions (like breathing and heartbeat), our Source OS runs automatically in the background.

We experience this automated system when we receive a strong gut feeling, sense danger, or experience déjà vu. We don't have to believe in (or be exploring) our spiritual gifts to receive Source communication. Our Source OS (inherent knowledge) includes:

1. **Source information.** Contains all the higher knowledge of Source (such as universal laws, spiritual truths, the creative process, and more).
2. **Spirit (soul) information.** Includes its history, abilities, frequency, and more.
3. **Source communication channels.** The spiritual gifts of seeing, hearing, smelling, tasting, touching, and knowing. Also, your direct link with Source.

We cannot change or delete our Source OS, but we can silence it by allowing the things we've learned to take priority over it. When we were born into this world, we were operating straight from our Source OS. If you have childhood memories of seeing spirits, talking to animals, knowing what others were about to say, dreams, or other experiences, it was your Source OS at work!

Our Source OS is free from prejudice, racism, hate, or other negative beliefs or emotions. (The negative we see in our world is learned knowledge or learned behavior.)

This inherent knowledge stays with us forever because it's part of our soul or spirit (not the physical brain). We cannot remove or change it.

Our spirit brings along inherent knowledge to assist us on our physical journey here on Earth. The knowledge in our Source OS can help us improve and balance our lives. It can assist us in our decision-making, parenting, beliefs, making friends, finding our life purpose, avoiding danger, living a happy life, and much more!

How Source OS Works With Other Systems

As mentioned in the first chapter, our Source OS is part of an automated creation system that brings about what we experience in our daily lives. This system includes:

1. **Inherent Knowledge (Source OS).** Inherent knowledge <u>cannot be changed</u>. We do not learn it . . . we remember it! We can view it as our spiritual mind. It is our <u>inside knowledge</u>.
2. **Learned Knowledge (training and experience).** Learned knowledge <u>can be changed</u>. This knowledge reflects our beliefs about ourselves and the world (based on what we've learned and experienced). We can view it as our knowledge mind. It is our <u>outside knowledge</u>.

3. **Subconscious Mind.** Our subconscious mind <u>can be refocused</u>. This part of the system creates what we experience in our daily lives. We give it instructions based on what we focus our energy and attention on every day. It is the <u>outward demonstration</u> of the instructions we have put into it.
4. **Conscious Choices**. Everything we think, say, do, and feel during our waking hours. (What we give our energy and attention to based on our Source OS and learned knowledge.) They are the <u>instructions we give to our subconscious mind</u>.

What we experience in our daily life is based upon using a balance of our Source OS and learned knowledge in our everyday decisions and actions. Why would we create and sustain an unhappy life on purpose? The answer is, <u>we</u> <u>wouldn't</u>. Most of us are unaware of what we are doing because we've been taught to rely on our learned knowledge (which we'll discuss in greater detail in the next chapter).

We begin acquiring learned knowledge at birth (and it continues throughout our lifetime). In the beginning, we process our training and experiences through our senses and our child's mind. Our beliefs become a mix of truths, false conclusions, and adopted perspectives. We then download these results over the top of our Source OS!

If we're not allowed to use (or even know about) our Source OS, we will rely upon our learned knowledge only. When we navigate through life relying solely on our learned knowledge, we edge out (or silence) our inherent knowledge.

These learned knowledge downloads slow down or place our Source OS in something similar to "sleep mode". Whatever unnecessary additions have been placed on top of our Source OS, and do not work in our best interest, are preventing us from accessing our inherent knowledge fully. Examples of these downloads are:

1. Beliefs instilled by home, school, or religion that you accepted (which are false or not beneficial).
2. Things you experienced (good and bad) and what you accepted as true from them.
3. Things you focus your time, energy, and attention on every day.

In other words, we override our inherent knowledge (Source OS) by substituting it with our learned knowledge. We learn to ignore our inherent knowledge. We are spiritual beings, living in a physical body, and we have cut off our spiritual side! This means we are operating with one of the three pieces (required for life balance) missing.

Our world reflects the consequences of this imbalance. There are many unhappy, afraid, depressed, suicidal, and lost people on Earth. They may be looking for someone to come along and "save" them or save their country. If **we** were using our Source OS, we would know we have the creative power to save ourselves, our countries, and the planet!

There must be balance in all things. What is balance in this case? Balance is using our spiritual knowledge and adjusting any learned knowledge that opposes our Source OS. Once we bring back the piece that has been missing (inherent knowledge), we will experience the balance that has been missing in our lives.

Adjusting Our Source OS

The good news is that our Source OS isn't broken or defective! There is nothing flawed or imperfect about it. We can change the stuff we've layered on top of it (learned knowledge) that doesn't serve our Highest Good. Once we clean up the added stuff (and be open to using our Source OS), we will experience a much different life than the one we've known before.

Our teachers taught us to rely on our learned knowledge and discouraged us from using (or even mentioning) our inherent knowledge.

OUR BUILT-IN SPIRITUAL KNOWLEDGE

They told us that using our learned knowledge would make us happy and prosperous in life. Perhaps we were told it would help us **make it through** life. Either way, if stress, drama, past hurts, or other negatives fill our lives, it's a sign that our way of going about things is unbalanced. Restated, our unique learned knowledge is our primary "go-to" method of dealing with life and the results are less than favorable.

Let's use the smartphone as an example. Think of your Source OS as a brand-new smartphone. It comes with a ton of valuable tools and quickly responds to your requests. Over time, you add apps, photos, and other stuff (learned knowledge) to your phone. Your new phone becomes slower and less efficient than when it was new. You realize you've added too much stuff on your phone for it to work the way you want it to. You decide what you need to keep, and delete rarely used apps (or the ones that didn't do what you thought they would). All the photos that aren't "keepers" you transfer to a computer or laptop for safekeeping. And just like that, your smartphone speed and efficiency increase again!

Apply the smartphone example when your life isn't working as well as you imagined it would. Once you realize your life isn't what you want it to be, decide what you want to keep, use, and remove.

Look at what isn't working (what you've accepted as true and what you give your energy to) and choose to change what is out of alignment with your Highest Good or opposes your Source OS. The goal is to use your inherent knowledge, learned knowledge that doesn't conflict with your Source OS, and make sure what you think, say, do, and feel is what you want in your life!

Strengthening Our Source OS

The best way to strengthen our connection to Source OS is by <u>using it</u> (practice). Spiritual knowledge and abilities are remembered and experienced. Reading a book or taking a class will help ignite the remembering, but only by <u>doing</u> will you strengthen the connection. Practice paying close attention to what you think, say, do, and feel during the day. Ensure your thoughts, words, actions, and emotions align with your desires. A future book in this series will delve into the power of words, thoughts, emotions, and actions. Meanwhile, here are a couple of key points to remember:

1. Words, thoughts, emotions, and actions have the power to create or destroy (**you** choose which).
2. Anything that comes after "I AM." must be positive!

OUR BUILT-IN SPIRITUAL KNOWLEDGE

Every time we talk about ourselves (or others), we are casting a spell! If we choose positive words, there will be a positive effect. Conversely, if we choose to use negative words, there will be a negative effect. When we're young, the adults in our life may cast spells on us with words like ugly, stupid, or clumsy. They may also harm us physically or mentally, and this makes us believe it is how things are or it's what we deserve.

As adults, we reinforce these spells daily with what we think, say, do, and feel! Whatever we learned about ourselves and the world as children continues to run on autopilot as adults. We continue to attract people and experiences into our lives (without knowing it) based on our childhood learned knowledge! Our learned knowledge can be helpful or harmful. The harmful aspects are why most people experience repeating cycles of financial difficulty, failed relationships, stress, drama, and more.

Another way we can strengthen our connection to our spiritual knowledge is to pay attention to any out-of-the-ordinary happenings. Write about them in your journal. Examples of these out-of-the-ordinary events may be when you:

1. Hear a song on the radio that reminds you of a person or event and you relive it like it happened yesterday.

2. Receive thoughts of a person you weren't thinking about, and they stay with you for a while.
3. See, hear, feel, or smell something that brings back memories of another time, place, or person.
4. Have a vivid dream and recall every detail.
5. Encounter an animal acting out of character, or it is paying close attention to you.

These examples show events that may occur with more attention given to your Source OS. Tip: If something strange occurs, and you think, "That was weird," journal about it. These happenings are spiritual communications and/or your spiritual abilities picking up on subtle clues from the universe. It's important to remember ALL of creation conspires to assist you in life.

The meanings (from the five examples above) may be: A deceased relative letting you know they are thinking about you; an experience you still need to learn something from (or let it go); another person is thinking about you; your dream gives you kudos or advice; or an animal is trying to deliver a message. The more you are open to experiencing the spiritual part of you, the stronger it will become.

Our Source OS is there as a helping tool and compass of sorts. We receive information designed to guide us, answer our questions, help us have a good life, stay safe, and much more.

Don't worry if using your spiritual abilities feels unfamiliar initially. It's just because you've not been using it for a while. Like riding a bicycle, it won't take long to get the hang of it again!

My Experience

Although I remember the spiritual happenings I had as a child, like many, learned knowledge replaced my Source OS. Anytime I revealed spiritual insights or knowing to others, it was quickly ignored, corrected, or dismissed. It became crystal clear my spiritual way of seeing or knowing things was not acceptable behavior. So, they trained me to conform to societal expectations and to silence my spiritual self.

I've learned it doesn't matter how long our Source OS has been snoozing. It's always running in the background, sending out this "ping" (like a homing beacon) to remind us of what we came here to do and learn. We can feel it in our bones, even though we may not be able to describe it or know what it means. The ping will grow stronger over time. It informs us of a greater purpose in life, urging us to act or make changes. This ping wakes us up from our slumber of spirit.

I refer to this ping as the "midlife crisis of spirit". Age has nothing to do with it. People are experiencing this at younger and younger ages.

It's the point at which we realize the world we live in isn't what we thought or hoped it would be. We start searching for something better or more "real". We also start feeling an inner prompting, navigating us toward higher things, truth, joyous things, etc.

My first strong ping came after being in my job for about nine years. I started seeing how my job and its culture were changing. I had not dealt with the long-term effects of my childhood. My life had been a series of repeated behaviors resulting in less-than-optimal results. In about two years, the "spinning my wheels" life reached its breaking point, which I refer to (in my memoir) as my crazy, white girl mental breakdown. After this event, I discovered why my life wasn't working and why I kept getting the same results. I began changing my beliefs (which changed my habits and actions) and using my Source OS again. All the good I've experienced since then has been because of my Free Will choice to change what wasn't working.

SPIRITUAL OS PRACTICES

The following practices will assist you in tuning into your inherent knowledge. Please read over each one (and the notes) before completing them. Set aside some quiet time to <u>do</u> them. Suggest doing one at a time with a break of one day in between.

OUR BUILT-IN SPIRITUAL KNOWLEDGE

Give yourself time to fully absorb the impact. Don't forget to write about your experience in your journal!

Practice: Stress Buster Breathing

When doing spiritual practices, it's easier to experience them when our body is relaxed and our mind is quiet. I highly recommend doing this breathing practice before completing each exercise in this book.

This practice is designed to help you:
Relax your body and quiet your mind so you can get the most out of each practice.
Release any stress you may be holding in your body.

When you can do this practice:
Before completing each exercise in this book.
Anytime you feel stressed, anxious, angry, sad, overwhelmed, etc. (Take a couple of minutes to do this simple practice and feel the stress melt away!)

Time needed: 5 minutes.

What you will need:

1. A quiet, comfortable, space.
2. Something comfortable to sit or lay on.

3. Your journal and something to write with.

<u>Reminder</u>:
Review the entire practice (including the notes) before completing this practice.

<u>Follow these steps</u>:

1. Sit or lay in a comfortable position.
2. **Breathe in.** Through your nose, slowly filling your belly with air.
3. **Breathe out.** Through your mouth, slow and easy, until your belly goes flat.
4. **Breathe in and visualize**: Breathing in white light and it filling your entire body from head to toe.
5. **Breathe out and visualize**: Exhaling any negative or stress that <u>may</u> be in your body.
6. **Continue cycles** of breaths and visualization until white light fills your entire body, and you feel relaxed and calm.

NOTE 1: Don't worry if you start feeling strange sensations or if you see or hear things. Just focus on your breathing and imagery.

NOTE 2: Stressed at work or home? Stuck in traffic? Worried about world events? Are people getting on your last nerve? Use this practice to help calm you! It's a quick and easy way to relieve stress!

NOTE 3: Breathing helps us to relax and calm. We get more oxygen and feel energized and alert. Breathing in white light is healing and cleansing. Exhaling is a release and detox.

NOTE 4: Complete the practice outside for an even more powerful experience!

Practice: The Remembering Activation

Bringing something new into your life is as simple as setting an intention and living your life as if it's already done. The Remembering Activation is an intention that wakes your inherent knowledge from sleep mode. Similar to us waking up, our spiritual self may feel groggy after a long slumber. It needs time and engagement to be wide awake. Remember, you've probably only used your inherent knowledge occasionally over the years. Think of this activation as morning coffee for your spiritual self!

<u>This practice is designed to help you</u>:
Set your intent to remember (and start using) your inherent spiritual knowledge. (When you do this, you are welcoming <u>back</u> into your life one-third of what helps you live a balanced life. You are also giving permission to receive information and insights through your spiritual or Divine Self.)

<u>When you can do this practice</u>:
You only have to do this practice once!

<u>Time needed</u>: 5 minutes.

<u>What you will need</u>:

1. A quiet, comfortable, space.
2. Something comfortable to sit or lay on.
3. Your journal and something to write with.

<u>Reminder</u>:
Review the entire practice (including the notes) before completing this practice.

<u>Follow these steps</u>:

1. Sit or lay in a comfortable position.

2. Close your eyes (optional) and surround yourself with white light.
3. **Breathe in**. Through your nose, slowly filling your belly with air.
4. **Breathe out**. Through your mouth, slow and easy, until your belly goes flat.
5. **Repeat** 4 cycles of deep breathing.
6. **Breathe out and say aloud**: "I am remembering my inherent knowledge with ease and grace."
7. **Breathe in and say aloud**: "I am."
8. **Continue cycles** of deep breathing until you are relaxed and feel you're finished.
9. **Give thanks** for the help in remembering!

NOTE 1: Using "I AM." in the practices is using the name of Spirit (God, Universe, Creation) to create. It also implies that whatever you are creating is already done (right now versus in the future)!

NOTE 2: Each person will have their own unique experience (each person receives exactly what they need). You may have a lot happen, nothing at all, or something in between. Trust the activation is working **in your time** and **in the best way for you**.

NOTE 3: As you remember your inherent knowledge and realize you're receiving guidance, you may feel a little strange. You are relying on your spiritual side more and it feels different from the logical brain you are used to using. You are growing!

NOTE 4: After completing the practice, remember to treat yourself kindly and allow any emotions, thoughts, or insights to come out. Eat healthy, drink filtered or spring water, and get good sleep.

NOTE 5: For an in-depth study of the use of "I AM." in this and other practices, please check out *Wishes Fulfilled* by Dr. Wayne Dyer.

NOTE 6: **Wait at least 4 days before moving on to the next chapter!** This is to allow time for your body, mind, and spirit to adjust.

NOTE 7: Be sure to write about your experiences over the next four days in your journal!

NOTE 8: Complete the practice outside for an even more powerful experience!

OUR BUILT-IN SPIRITUAL KNOWLEDGE

In this chapter, we went into detail about the inherent knowledge (Source OS) we are all born with and some ways it was silenced during our childhood. We also talked about how our inherent knowledge, learned knowledge, and the subconscious work together to create what we experience in our lives. We discovered how important our daily think, say, do, and feel is to creating the life we want versus the life we're experiencing today.

The best news from this chapter is your Source OS is always with you! It is your North Star or your compass. Only you can place limits on it (like your beliefs about it and your spiritual gifts). The inner promptings you keep receiving (to do certain things or change things) come from your Source OS! It's like a gentle nudge. Inherent knowledge speaks to your Highest Self, reminding you of your life's purpose to fulfill, achieve, and learn.

When you decide to return to your Source OS, doors will open, answers will come, and change will become a reality! To understand how the second part of this life-creating system works (for or against) our Source OS, let's explore our learned knowledge . . .

4
Our Learned Knowledge

*What we know may be our best friend . . .
or our worst enemy.*

Along with our inherent knowledge (Source OS), we're also born with the capacity to learn from our physical environment (learned knowledge). As we discovered in the previous chapter, there are four parts to our life-creating system:

1. Inherent knowledge
2. Learned knowledge
3. The subconscious mind
4. Our conscious choices

This chapter discusses the origins of our learned knowledge and how it works with the other parts of this system to create our daily life experiences.

Learned knowledge is everything we have learned and experienced since birth. It is how we develop our beliefs about ourselves, others, and how we view the world. It is what created our beliefs, personality, thought processes, and behaviors. Each of us has a unique set of learned knowledge. This uniqueness plays a major role in our understanding and using spiritual gifts. We continue to add to our learned knowledge over our lifetime, but it is our childhood learned knowledge that has the most lasting and profound affect on the rest of our lives.

Unlike our Source OS, we are able to change our learned knowledge. We change it to experience spiritual growth and improve our lives. Our learned knowledge may not be in alignment with our Source OS, so being able to change or revise it is crucial. For many of us, our learned knowledge conflicts with our inherent knowledge. We experience this conflict in the stress, drama, trauma, or other negatives in our daily life. This learned knowledge will stay with us until we decide we want to change it. No one can change it for us or force us to change it.

When we came into this world, we had our Source OS and our innate ability to learn through others and our experiences. Any hatred, racism, prejudice, or other negative beliefs we hold are learned knowledge! The negative beliefs about ourselves, others, or the world are learned (not inherent) knowledge!

If our learned and inherent knowledge was more in alignment, many of us wouldn't be experiencing such ongoing discontent with our lives! We wouldn't have to remember our inherent knowledge . . . we would be living it every day!

Sources of Learned Knowledge

Sources of learned knowledge include family make-up, socio-economic status, country of origin, parental occupations, and much more. These sources vary from person to person. To keep things simple, we'll use four major categories for this discussion: our parents and extended family, formal education, life experiences, and religion.

Parents and Family

What our family teaches us is based on their inherent and learned knowledge. How they teach us to handle daily living is rooted in their beliefs and behaviors. We observe and mirror their beliefs, behaviors, speech, and way of handling daily tasks.

Sociologist Morris Massey describes a period during our childhood training and experience as the Imprint Period. He describes this period for children (up to the age of seven) when we absorb everything around us like sponges and accept much of it as true.

He also explains how this confusion and blind belief can lead to trauma and other deep problems.

Massey also concludes that this period is when we learn our sense of right and wrong, good and bad. Knowing this information, we can see how crucial early training is for children.

Formal Education

The majority of children in the United States receive their formal education through public schools. They are required to complete twelve years of formal education. The public education system includes the federal government, teachers, school boards, and teachers' unions. These entities decide what children in public schools will learn. What they learn and experience during those twelve years will have a profound affect on their developing minds.

These curriculum decisions mainly exclude parental input. Public school curriculum focuses on rote learning (using the brain for memorization, routine, conformity, and repeatable tasks). Creativity or real-world experiences are limited. The quality of education a child receives varies between schools and school districts, even within the same city or state! This method of learning is reinforced in our children for twelve years!

Learning about inherent knowledge isn't part of what a student learns in public schools. Parents who want their child to learn about spiritual topics have a choice between enrolling them in a private school that teaches spiritualism, or home-school them. Public schools teach children to rely on their learned knowledge versus a balance between learned and inherent knowledge!

Life Experiences

Our foundational experiences (good and bad) form in childhood using our five senses. These experiences (combined with our training) helped create the beliefs we formed about life, ourselves, and the world. Many of the "experience beliefs" we developed during childhood are inaccurate and not aligned with our inherent knowledge.

We created beliefs when our ability to process information and experiences was still developing. As mentioned earlier, children take things at face value and absorb their environment like a sponge. They process everything through their child's mind, come to conclusions, then accept those conclusions as truth. The result is a mixture of truths, half-truths, and falsehoods. As we grow older, we realize and change some of our false beliefs (like Santa Claus). But some of the beliefs stick with us into adulthood.

Religion

Religious beliefs are formed by what we learn and experience while participating in church services, religious schools, or other church-related activities. Messages delivered by religious leaders have a major impact on our religious or spiritual belief system.

What a religious text or doctrine conveys as the proper way to think, act, and behave can also create beliefs not aligned with our inherent knowledge. When religious teachings don't align with our inherent knowledge, we begin doubting those teachings. We may even disconnect from religion because of this inner conflict between religion and Source OS.

For instance, let's say our religious text states we are sinners and imperfect. Our inherent knowledge (spiritual truths) tells us of perfect creation and having a divine spark of God within. At some point, these two opposing beliefs will clash! If you attended church as a child, and learned the "sinner doctrine," do you recall how you felt when you were first taught you were an imperfect sinner?

Important Note

Not all our training and experiences brought us positivity or were true. Not that our parents or other adults lied to us or meant to do us harm.

(Though we know some did.) The adults who taught us were just passing along what they had learned, experienced, and believed. (Much like how your parents passed along their genes to you.) Passing along beliefs and skills is fine as long as they work for you (versus against you).

Learned Experience Example

Let's just say when you were growing up, your parents argued often. They gave each other the cold shoulder or hurled negative words at each other. As a child, you witnessed this behavior and experienced how your mom and dad treated each other. At first, their behavior disturbed you, and you cried or became frightened. These experiences contradicted your innate knowledge (despite your unawareness). After a while (if their negative behavior continued), you didn't cry anymore. It no longer made you afraid. In your child's mind, you started believing it's just how moms and dads treat each other.

Once you've grown up, you live on your own as an adult. When you and your spouse get married, disagreements occur. Your belief is it's okay, because that's what your mom and dad did. Or perhaps you so disliked the constant arguing in your house growing up that you now reject any arguing whatsoever. You refuse to argue, ever. Neither one of these creates balance in your life. You're unhappy and life isn't what you thought it would be.

To find happiness, you must embrace positive beliefs about spousal treatment in a fulfilling relationship.

We are born with a clean slate for learning and trust that what we're being taught is best for us. We accepted all our training and experiences as truth and adopted them as our knowledge and beliefs. Each of us had a unique upbringing. No parents or siblings are the same. Some children experience normal childhoods while others go through horrific experiences. The result is a wide variety of beliefs and behaviors of future generations.

As adults, we have both positive and negative beliefs and behaviors. Whether they are positive or negative doesn't automatically make them true or good for us. We should always ask whether our beliefs are in alignment with our inherent knowledge. Here's an easy way to tell if your beliefs don't align with your Source OS: If your life is stressful, unhappy, or drama-filled, your learned knowledge (beliefs and behaviors) aren't in alignment with your inherent knowledge.

Let me be <u>very</u> <u>clear</u> here . . . Some things we believe to be true about ourselves and the world (based on our training and experience) are not serving our Highest Good. They cause our lives to be less than desirable. However, this doesn't mean all we've learned and experienced was for naught. Everything we've learned and experienced has given us unique skills and abilities to navigate our lives!

My Experience

I'd like to share an example from my personal experience to assist you in understanding how this all fits together. I grew up in an environment of abuse, poverty, addiction, and racism. Learning how to be quiet and invisible was one of my early lessons. My parents always complained about how hard and unfair life was. They complained about their lack of money and believed rich people made their money by taking advantage of others. I often heard adults using racial slurs and felt the hate coming out of their mouths. This (and more) was my learned knowledge.

As an adult, I wondered why my life wasn't happy, fulfilling, or prosperous. I followed what I had been taught to survive and succeed. My relationships were drama-filled and stressful. Both of my marriages failed. One day, the stress, drama, and failure that was my life came crashing down.

After this life-changing event, I realized a lot of the things I knew were rooted in false beliefs. The training passed down to me through the generations of my family helped create these false beliefs. The training I received from all the generations of all the families whom I learned from (teachers, babysitters, clergy, etc.), also helped create my false beliefs.

For thirteen years, I had been beating my head against a wall, relying on my training and being bewildered as to why it wasn't working. My confusion made me feel like I was doing something wrong or wasn't smart enough to create the life I wanted. After my mini mental breakdown, I learned why my life wasn't working. I had silenced my inherent knowledge and not all my learned knowledge aligned with my Source OS! Had I wanted to continue to live a life of abuse, poverty, addiction, and drama, my training would have been a perfect match. It was what my conditioning told me to do. I could have spent my life complaining, hating others, and avoiding responsibility for my circumstances. Fortunately, I didn't want to live my life like that.

According to one of the universal laws, lies or falsehoods are always revealed or exposed, leaving only the truth. The truth may be painful, but we choose whether we want to accept it (or ignore it) and stay in the comfort of our false illusions. I looked at my beliefs, rejected those that didn't serve my Highest Good, and replaced them with ones more aligned with my inherent knowledge.

Right about now, you may have lots of questions filling your mind. What about all the abuse, poverty, addiction, and racism you experienced growing up? Was there no point to it all? Why did you have to endure pain and misery as a child? Is it just the way life is?

Do we live the rest of our lives dependent on our learned knowledge, unaware of our inherent knowledge, and repeating the same old cycles that keep us unhappy, addicted, or poor?

What I've learned and experienced since my "epiphany moment" is that no one has to remain stuck. No, it's not just the way life is and a tough break for you. No, the pain, distrust, misery, delusion, and all the other lessons and emotions served a purpose. As an adult, I assisted people from diverse backgrounds who were homeless, addicted, abused, and hungry. The girl who once walked on eggshells (and learned to be "quiet as a church mouse") became a public speaker!

I found success at helping my clients because I understood. I knew what they were going through because I had experienced it myself. And most importantly, they knew I knew. It gave me a type of credibility and trust with the people I assisted. It's my belief that all I've learned and experienced growing up qualified me to do what I came here to do! I could have complained about life's unfairness. Instead, I decided to understand why I had my experiences and what it all meant. Connecting with people and sharing my knowledge of our spiritual nature was the result.

In this chapter, we explored learned knowledge and how it forms our beliefs about ourselves, others, and our world. We discovered that each person's unique learned knowledge contains both true and false beliefs. We now know how this uniqueness helps us understand and use our spiritual gifts.

The third part of the creation system involves our subconscious mind. The subconscious mind runs in the background, but has an immediate effect on our daily life. In the next chapter, we'll discover how we can gain control of something running on autopilot. We'll also learn to give a fresh set of operating instructions to our subconscious mind.

5
The Power of Our Subconscious Mind

*Chaos comes from the imbalance between
the body, mind, and spirit.*

So far we've discovered we came here with spiritual knowledge (Source OS) and the foundation of our learned knowledge developed during early childhood. This chapter explores the subconscious mind's role in the creation process. What does the subconscious mind do? How does it affect our everyday life? Do we have any power to change it? Answering these questions is the focus of this chapter.

It is crucial to understand the role the subconscious plays in the current state of our lives. If we're not happy with life, the cause is the instructions we give our subconscious mind! The subconscious mind:

1. Doesn't know truth from fiction.
2. Works all day, every day, to give you what you <u>ask</u> for.
3. Uses the focus of your energy and attention (your ask) as its operating instructions.

Let's examine each of these traits . . .

Doesn't know truth from fiction

The subconscious mind is simplistic because it takes things at face value. It passes no judgment, nor is it a detector of lies or truth. The subconscious mind takes the information it receives and uses it to create what we experience in life.

Works all day, every day, to give you what you <u>ask</u> for

The subconscious mind runs on autopilot (much like our breathing or heart beat). It never rests, has a day off, or takes a vacation. This part of our creative system monitors where we send our energy and attention every day (what we ask for) and creates it in real-time! It is an essential part of our creative ability. We cannot shut it off, but we can reprogram or refocus it by changing what we are asking for!

Uses the focus of your energy and attention (your ask) as its operating instructions

The subconscious mind creates our life experience based on what we focus our energy and attention on every day. We focus our energy and attention through our daily thoughts, words, actions, and emotions. These are the instructions we give our subconscious mind! These thoughts, words, actions, and emotions are based on our Source OS (which may be in sleep mode) and our learned knowledge. Remember, the subconscious mind doesn't know truth from fiction, so it assumes whatever you focus your time, energy, and attention on each day is what you want in your life.

Most of us were not trained to use our Source OS, so we think, say, do, and feel based upon our learned knowledge. As we've discussed, not all our learned knowledge is true or helpful. Do you perceive the potential negative impact on your life?

The subconscious mind has no interest in our beliefs about ourselves and others, our religion, how we handle daily life tasks, or how well we get along with others. Its only concern is what we give our energy and attention to every day. We give our energy and attention to things through our words, feelings, thoughts, and actions.

Consider the time you spend daily on your words, feelings, thoughts, and actions. Are they what you want to experience every day of your life?

There are mitigating circumstances why our body, mind, and spirit aren't operating in balance (disease, depression, etc.). As mentioned in previous chapters, most of us were not provided with education about our spiritual nature or how to use it. We learned to rely almost entirely on our learned knowledge. As a result, we may not know how to release past negative in order to stay healthy. We may not have the skills to change learned behaviors that are detrimental to our life. We now realize that not knowing this major reason has prevented us from living the life we imagined.

The subconscious mind is a complex, yet simple tool in the creative process. It is part of the "Ask, and it shall be given unto you" creative power of Source. The subconscious mind is one tool we can use with our creative power to work <u>for</u> us versus against us.

Examples of How the Subconscious Mind Works

When we first encounter this part of our creative system, it can be confusing. To comprehend how the subconscious mind creates our experiences, visualizing the process is beneficial.

Two examples demonstrate how individuals shape their life experience with money using their subconscious mind:

Example #1: Karly

Karly isn't aware she has a Source OS (like most of us). She learned that money is hard to earn and even harder to keep. She witnessed her parents struggle with paying bills and providing enough food or other necessities for their family.

- Inherent Knowledge (Source OS): There is no lack. The universe is full of abundance. Source did not create lack.
- Learned Knowledge (Beliefs): "There is never enough money." "I'm always broke."
- Conscious Choices: Karly is always worried about paying her bills (think). She talks about how broke she is to her friends and family (say). She does not manage her money well and spends money on impulse items (do). Her self-view is incapable of managing money and not smart enough to figure out what she is doing wrong (feel).

- Subconscious Mind: "Karly wants to worry about money and likes to tell her friends about her money struggles. She wants to never have enough money and feel unhappy, sad, or depressed about it. Okay, I got this!"

Karly may stay in her low-paying job or find a better-paying job. Whether she receives a raise at her current job or gets a bump in pay at a new job, she soon discovers she still doesn't make enough money! She continues to complain about her financial misery and spends what little extra money she has on items she believes will bring her a little happiness or fortune (like lottery tickets).

Every decision she makes is based on her learned knowledge. Karly's money cycle continues for years. She wonders why she must continue to struggle with money. Karly struggles with money because her daily thoughts, words, actions, and feelings around money focus on her lack of money!

Example #2: Ken

Ken discovered he has a Source OS and understands some of the spiritual truths about money, prosperity, and abundance. He learned that money is hard to earn and even harder to keep.

Ken also witnessed his parents struggle with paying bills and providing enough necessities for their family.

- Inherent Knowledge (Source OS): There is no lack. The universe is full of abundance. Source did not create lack.
- Learned Knowledge (Beliefs): "There is never enough money." "I'm always broke."
- Conscious Choices: Ken realizes some of his money beliefs (and actions) caused his financial struggles. He knows he has to do something different if he wants to get different results. Ken takes action and changes his belief that he's always broke. His new belief is, "I am attracting more than enough money." He focuses his mind on having more than enough money to pay all his bills (think). His money talk (to himself and with his friends and family) is positive (say). Ken takes a class on budgeting to understand where he spent his money in the past (do). With new-found confidence, he envisions turning his finances around and experiencing abundance.
- Subconscious Mind: "Ken wants to attract more than enough money. He enjoys being able to tell others he's doing well with his finances. He feels good about attracting money into his life. Okay, I got this!"

Ken won't stay in his current job. It's not in alignment with his new belief of attracting "more than enough". He will most likely find a better-paying job he likes. With his new budgeting skills (and new money belief), Ken will soon discover he has more money than ever before! Ken continues to think about his money prospects in a positive way (think). He has positive things to say when discussing money with others (say). He makes better financial decisions than he did before (do). Ken is happier about his money story and believes he has the power to make his positive progress permanent (feel). Ken no longer struggles with money because his daily thoughts, words, actions, and feelings around money focus on abundance and prosperity!

There is a significant contrast between the two individuals in these examples. Both had the same learned knowledge about money, but one had discovered their inherent knowledge and realized he could use it to assist him in changing his "money story".

We can tell if we're giving our subconscious mind the proper instructions by what we are experiencing in everyday life! If you face challenges in finance (or any aspect of life), observe your thoughts, words, actions, and emotions regarding it daily. It's an easy way to see what you are doing to bring about what you're experiencing.

My Experience

I grew up in a poor family. My dad had a low-paying job. In the beginning, my mom stayed at home to raise her children. When she started working, she also had a low-paying job. Discussions about money in our household were filled with negativity. My parents blamed other people, high prices, and the government for our lack of money. In truth, the cause of our money problems was one parent addicted to alcohol.

When I graduated high school, I decided I wouldn't live my life working dead-end jobs and struggling as my parents had. My first job paid decent money, and I worked my way up and received steady raises. However, my rebellion over never being able to buy anything other than necessities created a reactionary habit. If I lacked funds, I'd use a credit card for purchases.

So, I created this cycle of charging up credit cards, paying them off, then maxing them out again. This cycle didn't have any serious consequences (other than my credit score), but the monthly payments took a sizeable chunk out of my monthly earnings. At one point I had lost my job, wasn't able to make the monthly payments, and had to file for bankruptcy! I had to figure out why I was abusing my credit cards. I realized it was the money story I had accepted as true growing up.

If there is never enough money, I'll just supplement my earnings with credit cards. If I don't have the money for that, I'll just charge it. This is how I dealt with the poverty mentality I learned as a child.

Rarely did I receive what I wanted as a child due to our financial state, so I ensured I obtained it as an adult. Sounds crazy, right? My learned knowledge and my attention created my credit card habits. I spent so much money on minimum monthly payments, I had very little money left over each month. My subconscious mind gave me what I was asking for. It ensured a perpetual lack of funds!

In this chapter, we gained a clearer understanding of how the subconscious mind works. We also discussed how it interacts (through us) with our learned knowledge and our Source OS. The instructions we give our subconscious mind are super-important. We also discovered how small a part our Source OS may be playing in those instructions.

We are the primary creative force in our lives and the choices we make every day determine our life experience. Our daily think, say, do, and feel ensures what we will experience tomorrow. What we give our energy and attention to (based on our Source OS and learned knowledge) is the last piece of the life-creating process and awaits us in the next chapter . . .

6

It Matters What You Think, Say, and Do!

You are the creative source of your life.

It may seem as if we have no control over built-in operating systems, what we learned, and programs running in the background. Nothing could be further from the truth. The last part of this system (conscious choices) is how we control the entire system to benefit our life!

In this chapter, we will take a sobering look at conscious choices. We'll also uncover what drives our choices and how to use them to create the results we wish to experience in our life. Understanding how our choices affect each part of this system, we realize why some parts of our lives work well and others don't. We also see why some results of our decisions are always positive, while others have negative outcomes that keep repeating throughout our life.

What are Conscious Choices?

Conscious choices are the choices we make while we are awake, aware, or alert. *The Cambridge Dictionary* defines conscious as, "Awake, aware of what is happening around you, and able to think." We make hundreds of conscious decisions each day from the time we wake until we fall asleep again. Decisions include what we eat, activities we do, choosing what to wear, and much more.

Most of our decisions take little mental effort because they've become habits developed over time (run on autopilot). Some habits include when we wake up, go to work, eat, sleep, and more. Perhaps we don't choose these decisions because we perform them without thinking. However, deferring to habit is a decision in itself. Relying on our habits is easier and more comfortable.

For example, Rita has a habit of eating fast food during her workweek. Over the last five years, she has gained about ten pounds each year. She's not happy buying larger-sized clothes and doesn't have as much energy as in the past. The last time she saw her doctor, he advised her to cut down on her trips to the drive-thru. But Rita continues to consume fast food because it's easier than packing a lunch. She continues to gain weight and feel less energetic. It's become a downward spiral. At some point, Rita will have to either pack her lunch or continue to gain weight and experience her health decline.

IT MATTERS WHAT YOU THINK, SAY, AND DO!

It's not always easy to break a habit. Some habits are more difficult to change than others. Past behavior shows the probabilities of future behavior. People do not change. It sometimes takes a life-changing event or wake-up call to cause them to change. An Anaïs Nin quote sheds light on this phenomenon: "And the day came when the risk to remain tight in a bud was more painful than the risk it took to blossom." At some point, the pain of change is far less than the pain of repeating the same old cycles.

In a nutshell, conscious choices are everything we think, say, do, and feel during our waking hours. They are what we give our energy and attention to every day. Yes, we make choices and are responsible for all our thoughts, words, actions, and feelings. No one can force our actions, words, thoughts, or emotions (unless we're under duress). We have the power to choose our thoughts, words, actions, and emotions. We choose what will receive our energy and attention.

Let's say Carlos and his supervisor disagree about how to complete a project. During their discussion, Carlos' supervisor becomes angry and tells Carlos to stop complaining. He also tells Carlos to complete the project according to plan, or he will pull him off the job and put someone else in charge. Carlos becomes angry with his supervisor over this exchange. He remains angry for the rest of the day as he continues working with his crew on the project.

Did Carlos' boss <u>make</u> him angry? What caused his anger? Was it his supervisor's words, the tone, or something else? Did Carlos have to get angry? To answer these questions, we must determine the reason behind Carlos's choice to become (or stay) angry.

What Drives Our Conscious Choices?

Our conscious choices are driven by our inherent and learned knowledge. As mentioned before, if we haven't learned to use our Source OS, we only have our learned knowledge to rely on. When we operate from our learned knowledge (training and experiences), we don't always get positive results. So, our reliance on it persists, because it remains our sole resource (or so we assume).

Our learned knowledge includes how we do things, what we believe, our culture, our values and ethics, how we interact with others, and much more. It also includes all our good and bad habits, things that remind us of bad experiences, and how we view other people and cultures. Therefore, it's crucial to discover which parts are serving us well and which are causing lack, stress, drama, or trauma in our lives. It's also why we need to experience our Source OS and begin using it again to help us discover better ways to make conscious choices. Let's return to our example of what happened to Carlos . . .

Carlos became angry because of a negative conversation with his boss. Was there a lack of good communication? Maybe. Did his boss use a threatening tone or words? It appears he did. This still doesn't explain why Carlos became angry and let this interaction affect his entire day. Does Carlos' ethics tell him a supervisor should never ridicule an employee in front of others? Is his culture telling him men should show each other respect? Did Carlos feel his job competency was being questioned?

Perhaps someone taught Carlos that employees receive poor treatment by people in positions of power. If we were to speculate, we could conclude all Carlos had to rely on was his learned knowledge. He wasn't aware of his inherent knowledge. Carlos may have several beliefs or experiences that helped fuel the anger he felt over the conversation.

How could Carlos have reacted differently? He could have decided not to remain angry for the rest of his day. He could have decided he would not stress over it. Had Carlos known how to use his Source OS, he would have known how (or when) he allowed others to make him feel a certain way.

How to Use Our Choices to Create

Learned knowledge is only half of the tools we need to help us create the life we want! Not having (or not knowing how to use) our inherent knowledge is like having a job that requires two volumes of operating instructions, but we only have one. Yeah, we can get by and hope nothing disastrous happens, but then we are just crossing our fingers and hoping for the best. The best recipe for changing what isn't working is equal parts learned knowledge, inherent knowledge, and daily actions. They will assist us in creating a life that is more balanced and positive!

In the third chapter, we talked about the power of words, thoughts, actions, and feelings. These daily tools create our life experiences. We don't have to remember everything in our Source OS before we transform our thoughts, speech, behavior, and emotions! Remember, the operating system (Source OS) and programs (learned knowledge and the subconscious mind) are still running in the background. Focus on changing the ones you can (learned knowledge and subconscious programming) and begin opening up and learning more about your inherent knowledge.

So, we don't have to wait until we discover all that our Source OS offers. We begin by asking, "What isn't working?" and focus our energy and attention on what we think, say, do, and feel around the answer to change it.

IT MATTERS WHAT YOU THINK, SAY, AND DO!

We change it by making a new belief habit and practicing it until it is part of who we are and becomes automatic! Chapters eight and nine will cover recognizing and changing beliefs.

My Experience

Several years after becoming an adult, I realized how my thoughts, words, feelings, and actions had created misery in my life. My beliefs about money landed me in credit card debt. Experiences I'd had with men left me distrusting of them. I was unemployed for months and had a hard time getting into college. No matter what I tried, just about every part of my life was failing. I started believing there was something wrong with me. That I wasn't capable of bettering myself or getting ahead.

After reading several self-help books, I realized the problem wasn't me, but the tools given to me to work with. Yes, I was making the choices, but borrowed beliefs fueled most of those choices. My training had conditioned me to rely on acquired knowledge and prevented me from using my inherent knowledge. So, my think, say, do, and feel was based on false beliefs and training. I had been using a set of instructions that hadn't worked for my family, but expected them to work for me!

Realizing I couldn't just make different decisions and my problems would go away, I decided I had to reprogram the instructions that ran my think, say, do, and feel. So, I started looking at my beliefs. I identified the ones causing the most damage in my life and picked one to change. After I'd changed the first one, I went back to my list and picked another one to change. I repeated the process multiple times until my thoughts, words, actions, and feelings changed.

In this chapter, we learned what our conscious choices are. We discovered how our choices are the key ingredient in a four-part system used to create what we want to experience in life. We understand why what we think, say, do, and feel each and every day has made the life we are experiencing. We realized the importance of paying close attention to our thoughts, words, actions, and emotions throughout the day.

We now know changing our habits requires a glimpse into our Source OS. There, we will find guidance in the spiritual truths. Most of us did not learn these spiritual truths because we learned to rely on our learned knowledge. Some of these truths may be familiar to you if you've attended any alternative or spiritual-based churches.

7
Truths We Were Never Taught

The people no longer recognized The Truth within them through the smoke and illusion of their indoctrination.

There are universal laws or spiritual truths that rule our existence here on Earth (much like the law of gravity or action/reaction). Whether we believe in them is of no consequence . . . they are still in effect. These laws or truths, when followed and respected, create harmony in our lives. When ignored or abused, they cause chaos and imbalance. The spiritual truths in this chapter are part of the inherent knowledge hidden from humanity for millennia.

In the third chapter, we discussed that the inherent knowledge we came with (Source OS) is still present and contains truths that are non-changeable. There are things we believe are true, then there is The Truth (inherent knowledge).

Most of our beliefs we adopted from others. Some of these beliefs aren't bringing about positive results in our life and are opposite of The Truth. This is why our lives aren't working out the way we want them to. Some truths we'll discuss are:

1. You are never alone.
2. You are perfect.
3. You are worthy.
4. You are loved.
5. You have Free Will.
6. You have help.
7. You are an integral part of life.
8. You are safe and protected.
9. You are a creator.
10. You are unique.
11. You can choose any moment to change.
12. Who you are never changes.
13. True happiness comes from Within.
14. The past belongs in the past.
15. What we see in our world reflects our beliefs, hopes, fears, etc.
16. Everything you have learned and experienced in life has made you uniquely qualified to do what you came here to do and experience.
17. Coincidence does not exist.
18. You were born with spiritual gifts.

19. A person cannot be condemned to hell.
20. Balance is how things operate.

While reading about each spiritual truth, write in your journal about any thoughts, feelings, or emotions you notice.

You are never alone.

We feel alone when we believe ourselves to be separate from the rest of creation (other people, animals, nature, and even our spiritual self). When we rely solely on our knowledge mind, we become estranged from our spiritual self. We suffer the results of living illusions created by our false beliefs.

The Spirit That Moves in All Things (Source energy, creative energy, the source of All That Is) never abandons us. It is we who forget and feel unworthy of support, inner strength, or beauty. Connecting with our spiritual self ensures we will always feel loved, cared for, and part of the whole. Our spiritual connection (Source OS) is within us! We don't need to go looking for it outside ourselves. It's not <u>out there</u> somewhere. It is right here, housed within your physical body.

<u>Consider</u>: Each part of creation (including us) is an important part of the whole. Our thoughts, words, actions, and emotions have an impact on ourselves and the world. Imagine how good it would feel to really know in our hearts we are not alone!

You are perfect.

You were created perfect. The same universal source or higher power that created you is perfect. You lack nothing. Everything you need is inside you! Our body is self-sufficient. The way its systems run is wondrous. All we have to do is give it food, water, air, sun, and exercise.

The training and experiences we received from our parents, extended family, teachers, religious leaders, and others led us to believe we were not perfect. We learned we may one day (if we're good enough and sacrifice enough) be close to perfect.

<u>Consider</u>: If we believe God created us (and it was good), how can we also believe we are imperfect, damaged, or flawed? How could a perfect universe create imperfection? Please dedicate time to reflect and write about these questions.

You are worthy.

We are all worthy! No person is better than another. If a person believes they are better (or less) than others, it is part of their learned knowledge. We have experiences in life that make us believe we're not worthy (such as trauma, religion, abuse, etc.). Regardless of our financial or social status, health, beliefs, achievements, etc., everyone deserves to be recognized as worthy.

Consider: If we are all created perfect, then why wouldn't we be worthy? If we are not worthy, why were we given spiritual gifts, unique skills, and experiences to share with the world?

You are loved.

You are very loved . . . always! Love yourself as you are loved! Then, you'll love others and see love in the world.

If you were raised in the Christian faith, you might recall the Sunday School hymn *Jesus Loves the Little Children*. If you believe in this faith, then we are always the children of God, no matter what age we attain. We are always loved, even if we do not love ourselves. If you do not believe in God, know the universe, the creative Source, and your soul or spirit love you.

Consider: You came into this world filled with unconditional love! If we are created perfect and worthy, would the creative Source withhold love? Do you believe Source or Creator behaves as humans do and withdraws its unconditional love (or returns it) at any time?

You have Free Will.

You have Free Will to create or change your life. The choices you make are your responsibility. You cannot blame their outcome on others. You cannot change others (law of Free Will). Trying to change or control others is a fool's errand. We can only control our own lives. We choose how (or if) others affect us (**make** us mad, sad, etc.). Letting go of the desire to control or change others enables us to focus on ourselves and cultivate a better, happier life. Most people do what they know how to do. We are all at varying levels of understanding about ourselves and our spiritual potential.

Consider: You have the power to make decisions about your life. Spirit (or universe) doesn't interfere with your life. You're not a puppet on spiritual strings, with no control over what happens to you.

You have help.

We are not alone in this world. We have help from the universe or Source. All we have to do is **ask**! Ask the universe, angels, God, Gaia, Higher Self, or Source (or whatever your belief dictates). Pray, meditate, give thanks, etc.

We have so much help (higher power, guardian angels, archangels, Higher Self, creation, or whatever you believe in). Set your intent, ask for help, then get to work. Doors will open for you that were once closed, and almost immediately you'll start to notice your life changing. A Quaker proverb states, "As you pray, move your feet." It means ask for help, then do your part by taking action.

Consider: You have help from inside and outside of yourself. When we ask for help, all of creation conspires to assist us.

You are an integral part of life.

You matter just as everyone and everything else matters! Life includes all of creation, and you are an essential piece. Everything you've experienced, learned, and overcome has prepared you to live your purpose in this life. You have everything you need! There's no reason to hesitate. You are ready to dive in!

Consider: Everyone and everything matters. You are part of the web of life or the entire universe.

What each of us does has a positive or negative affect on the whole. Every part of creation matters! You are important to the balance of the universe. This is the essence of true equality.

You are safe and protected.

We're not thrown out into the world to fend for ourselves. We are all watched over all of our days. Each of us has a guardian angel and a protector whose job it is to ensure our safety. Believing in these things isn't required for them to be true. Regardless, your safety is assured. Pretty cool!

Some or most of our experiences, beliefs, and training make us feel insecure, unworthy, or afraid. We feel fear when we don't believe we are safe, or when we allow outside forces to convince us we are in danger all the time (TV, news reports, social media, politicians, etc.).

Consider: You have other spirit beings who watch over and protect you (angels, high spirit beings, guardian angels, protectors, guides, etc.). Have you experienced a life-threatening situation where time slowed, you watched the chaos unfold, then you walked away unscathed?

You are a creator.

Each of us has a spark of God within us (a piece of the creative or universal Source). This means you have the power to create, heal, and work miracles. We use our Free Will to create through our choices and intent. What we think, say, do, and feel is part of our built-in creative system. The intent behind our think, say, do, and feel gives us the power to create or destroy.

Consider this: You have the power to create your life, help create a better world, and heal yourself and others. Jesus (the Son of God in *The Holy Bible*) did not come to Earth to show us all the things he could do. He came here to demonstrate what each of us has the power to do!

You are unique.

No one has the exact skills and abilities as you! Your qualifications uniquely align with your purpose (what you feel drawn to do or decide you want to do). Every person brings distinct gifts to share with the world. What you have to share is important! Be yourself and don't worry about what others want you to be.

Consider: From the moment of your conception, you have had development, training, and experiences unique only to you. There is no one quite like you! The world would suffer a significant loss without you!

You can choose any moment to change.

You don't have to wait until tomorrow, next week, or the new year. You can choose any moment to release the past and start creating the life you want. One reason we stay stuck is, even though we may not like how our life is going, it's familiar . . . even comfortable! We kind of know what to expect. For our life to change, we must step outside the familiar or comfortable.

Consider: What is one positive change you could make in your life right now? How would your life be different?

Who you REALLY are never changes.

You are a spiritual being, living in a physical body, experiencing life on Earth. You're here to learn, grow, experience, and have fun along the way. Your spirit never dies. It is eternal and carries with it inherent spiritual knowledge.

We can change anything about our life and our beliefs. We have the power to remodel or makeover the life we're experiencing right now.

Consider: Imagine if you embraced your spiritual side right now. How much better would your life be in three months if you were happier, less stressed, and more abundant?

What positive results would your decisions create in your life if they were based on a balance of spiritual and learned knowledge?

True happiness comes from Within.

True happiness comes from loving yourself, taking care of yourself, choosing happiness, and accepting any joy that comes your way. It is a state of mind using a balance of learned and inherent knowledge.

Whatever is on the inside attracts what we experience in life. It does not come from the outside. Happiness is fleeting and fickle when we rely on it to come from outside sources (other people, achievements, jobs, relationships, etc.).

<u>Consider</u>: Imagine a life filled with happiness, where your self-esteem soars and love radiates within you and towards the world. How would that feel?

The past belongs in the past.

The best thing we can do with the past is learn from it, forgive ourselves, forgive others (if possible), and release any negative emotions or beliefs related to it. The longer we hold on to the past, the longer we relive it and repeat it. This causes us to attract similar experiences and people.

Letting the past go enables us to fully experience the present and eagerly anticipate the future. After the past is released, the dark clouds that once overshadowed our waking hours lift. The heavy ball and chain that drained our energy and zest for life fall away.

<u>Consider</u>: The past should stay in the past. It is where it lives and belongs. Only you can bring the past into the present.

What we see in our world reflects our beliefs, hopes, fears, etc.

We are creators and an integral part of the whole. What we do affects others and everything around us. It's like a fly hitting a spider's web, causing the whole web to vibrate. Or a rock hitting the water and the ripples spreading out a great distance.

This reflection is clear in our world today. The negatives of hate, prejudice, racism, bullying, ego, greed, and fear have transformed many countries. We have allowed governments, news media, social media, peers, education systems, and others to fill us with fear, frustration, and anger. The more we give this negativity our energy and attention, the stronger it grows. The best way to heal ourselves and the world is to replace the fear with positive.

Focus on yourself first, then your family, friends, neighbors, and your community. Don't allow yourself to be sucked in to the constant fear mongering.

<u>Consider</u>: What we think, say, do, and feel affects everyone and everything. Words, thoughts, actions, and emotions have the power to create or destroy.

Everything you have learned and experienced in life has made you uniquely qualified to do what you came here to do and experience.

Nothing you've learned or experienced is wasted. It's all part of your unique self. It's all useful for living life. There are reasons you learned and experienced what you have. You may not understand it at the present moment, and that's okay. We are all here to learn, have fun, experience, and find fulfilling purpose in life.

<u>Consider</u>: What are the odds of someone else having the exact upbringing, training, experiences, and qualifications as you?

Coincidence does not exist.

When we decide to do something (set our intent) and ask for help, <u>all</u> of creation conspires to assist us! Songs will play on the radio that remind us of something, someone, or answers questions we have.

We'll hear the same advice from multiple people in a short time. Animals appear and pay special attention to us. We may see pictures in the clouds. These are not coincidences, but synchronicity! Our intent and ask starts everything in motion. Creation conspiring to assist us is proof that we are not alone!

<u>Consider</u>: How often have you viewed an out of the ordinary experience as mere coincidence? Write about any that come to your mind.

You were born with spiritual gifts.

Everyone is born with a Source OS (inherent knowledge) that includes all the spiritual gifts. We can see, hear, taste, touch, smell, and know more than we believe we can. These abilities assist us in life and in living our purpose. All it takes is being open to remembering and reawakening your inherent knowing.

<u>Consider</u>: How would your life be different if you developed your gift of knowing?

A person cannot be condemned to hell.

When we die, we return to our original form, which is spirit. Our body returns to the Earth and our spirit (soul) returns to Source or Creation.

Hell is not a physical location, but a state of being. Purgatory is being separated from Source or God. If any spirit desires (chooses by Free Will) to return to Source, it shall be.

Consider: What are your beliefs about hell? What do you believe a person would have to do to deserve being condemned to hell for all eternity? Do you believe Source/Creation (which is all loving) would grant you only one chance (life) to prove you are worthy of heaven? How bad would you have to mess up your one chance in order to be stripped of your Free Will to choose to still go to "heaven"?

Balance is how things operate.

Balance is equal usage and nurturing of our body, mind, and spirit. Too much use of one, or lack of use in another, causes imbalance. For example, if we spend all our time improving our mind, but neglect our body, we create an imbalance between the two.

Consider: How many areas of your life are unbalanced at the moment?

My Experience

My childhood taught me not to trust adults because of the way some adults treated me growing up. It wasn't until I was an adult that I realized not **all** adults were untrustworthy. I believed I didn't have good looks, so I did my best to be smart and funny. Those were my coping mechanisms.

In my childhood, silence and unquestioning obedience were the norm, driven by the fear of severe consequences. As an adult, I let others dictate my actions against my own will. My self-esteem was very low. I desired love, but attracted the wrong individuals. It took me years to figure out everything, learn to speak up, refuse unwanted things, and realize self-esteem comes from within.

Lessons were slow in coming as I learned to live on my own as an adult. More lessons came after I had my semimental breakdown. It wasn't until I starting experiencing my inherent knowledge that I realized my learned knowledge wasn't helping me succeed. I finally understood my beliefs were ones I had accepted as true, or adopted from other people. They were not my own and often conflicted with spiritual truths and Universal Law. Relying on spiritual truths has led me to my greatest epiphanies in life.

SPIRITUAL TRUTHS PRACTICES

These practices will help you understand your beliefs and how they line up with spiritual truths. You will also set your intent to be open to learning more about your inherent knowledge.

Exercise: Truths Free Write

As we've discussed in previous chapters, our current beliefs don't always align with our inherent knowledge. This misalignment is reflected in our daily life experience. If you're unhappy, stressed, angry, worry about money, hate your job, or have too much drama in your life, it's because your learned and inherent knowledge are at odds.

This exercise is designed to help you:
Discover which of your learned beliefs are not in alignment with your inherent knowledge. This will help you pinpoint the ones causing discord in your life.

When you can do this exercise:
This exercise only has to be done once!

Time needed: 30 minutes.

What you will need:

1. A quiet, comfortable space where you can read and write.
2. Your journal and something to write with.

Reminder:

Review the entire practice (including the notes) before completing this practice.

Follow these steps:

1. Sit in a comfortable position.
2. **Breathe in.** Through your nose, slowly filling your belly with air.
3. **Breathe out.** Through your mouth, slow and easy, until your belly goes flat.
4. **Repeat** 4 cycles of deep breathing (or until you feel relaxed).
5. Go back and reread each truth from this chapter. As you read each one, ask yourself these questions about each truth:
   - Do I believe this truth? If not, what do I believe?
   - Where does this belief come from?
   - Who taught me this belief?

- What experience did I have that formed this belief?
6. When you've finished, close your journal and give thanks for any insights you had.

NOTE 1: Be sure to write about any experiences you have in the next 24 hours in your journal!

NOTE 2: **Wait at least one day before doing the next (or any other) practice!** This is to allow your body, mind, and spirit time to adjust.

Practice: Source Intention

After discovering which of our beliefs are out of alignment with our inherent knowledge, it's important to start learning more about (and trusting) the knowledge that is already inside us. This is a way of slowly integrating our inherent knowledge back into our lives and strengthening our long-neglected spiritual self.

This practice is designed to help you:
Set your intent to learn more about, trust, and use your inherent knowledge.

<u>When you can do this practice</u>:
You only have to do this practice once!

<u>Time needed</u>: 5 minutes.

<u>What you will need</u>:

1. A quiet, comfortable space.
2. Something comfortable to sit or lay on.
3. Your journal and something to write with.

<u>Reminder</u>:
Review the entire practice (including the notes) before completing this practice.

<u>Follow these steps</u>:

1. Sit or lay in a comfortable position.
2. **Breathe in**. Through your nose, slowly filling your belly with air.
3. **Breathe out**. Through your mouth, slow and easy, until your belly goes flat.
4. **Repeat** 4 cycles of deep breathing (or until you feel relaxed).
5. **Breathe out and say**: "I am trusting my Highest Self."
6. **Breathe in and say**: "I am."

7. **Continue cycles** of deep breathing until you feel you're finished.

NOTE 1: You can also say, "I am trusting my Divine Self. I am." OR "I am trusting my inherent knowledge. I am."

NOTE 2: You can repeat the "I am." statement throughout your period of deep breathing.

NOTE 3: Using "I AM." in the practices is using the name of Spirit (God, Universe, Creation) to create. It also implies that whatever you are creating is already done (right now versus in the future)!

NOTE 4: For an in-depth study of the use of "I AM." in this and other practices, please check out *Wishes Fulfilled* by Dr. Wayne Dyer.

NOTE 5: **Wait at least 4 days before doing the next (or any other) practice!** This is to allow your body, mind, and spirit time to adjust.

NOTE 6: Be sure to write about any experiences you have over the next four days in your journal!

In this chapter, we discussed some of the spiritual truths that are in play in our daily lives. Knowing these truths can help us understand how our learned knowledge may not align with our inherent knowledge. Once we uncover any inconsistencies, we are better prepared to choose and change any belief that isn't serving our Highest Good. First, let's examine our beliefs in greater detail.

8
What Do You Believe?

You are whatever you believe.

So far, we've learned how we formed our beliefs and the part our beliefs play in our everyday lives. We discovered we adopt the beliefs of others as our own, take them with us into adulthood, where the not-so-good ones wreak havoc on our day-to-day lives. Now we will discuss how many of our beliefs are false. We'll seriously evaluate our beliefs and identify those that require revision.

Most of us carry a lot of false beliefs because someone taught us untruths. We came to immature conclusions about our experiences when we were children. We even generalized those conclusions (rich people are bad). Perhaps our parents, other adults, or our peers ridiculed us when we did not conform to accepted norms, so we "went along to get along".

(If you want to explore beliefs and how they are formed in more detail, I highly recommend reading the book *The Four Agreements* by Don Miguel Ruiz.)

As adults, we still face ridicule, bullying, and peer pressure if we push back against the system (or don't go along with what the accepted behavior is) at any time. Have you ever been labeled as strange or different in the past? In today's environment, ridicule can come not only from adults and peers in our life but also from social media, mainstream media, and publications!

As we covered earlier, all our experiences and training form our learned knowledge. This doesn't stop after childhood. If we expose ourselves to certain beliefs (and entertain those beliefs), we adopt them into our daily lives. We then change what we are creating in our lives. Even as adults, we must remain vigilant to ensure we adopt new positive (versus negative) beliefs. But how can we tell the difference?

The easiest way to distinguish between positive and negative beliefs is to pay attention to how they make your body feel. Check if they are in alignment with your Source OS and assess the current condition of your life. Let's say you are watching a news story. Does the story cause you to be afraid, happy, sad, or depressed? Pay attention to what is being said. Are their words ridiculing people or behaviors? Do they demonize certain people?

Is this news source repeating the same story (in different ways) over and over, week after week, month after month? Are their news stories aligned with inherent or learned knowledge?

We must remember words, thoughts, actions, and emotions are powerful! They have the power to create beautiful things or to destroy them. We choose what we will use ours for, creation or destruction. Our think, say, do, and feel are shaped by our beliefs. Beliefs are learned behavior formed by our training and experiences. The more we learn about and use our inherent knowledge, the more we will choose beliefs aligned with it.

Let's examine our beliefs and determine:

1. What are our beliefs? Our beliefs are what we think is true about ourselves, others, money, relationships, religion, health, and the world.
2. What beliefs did we borrow from others? Do we have beliefs that aren't serving our Highest Good or are making our lives stressful or unhappy?
3. Which beliefs deviate from Universal Law or spiritual truths?

Every belief that opposes our Source OS (which includes universal laws and spiritual truths) makes it harder to discover our inherent abilities.

Each opposing belief makes it more difficult to realize that happy, fulfilling life we want, and can accomplish. We adopted our beliefs when we agreed with them and accepted them as truth. Some beliefs served us in the past, but are no longer doing so.

For example, when you were a child, you may have been told the story of Santa Claus and how he delivered presents for Christmas. You believed in Santa Claus because you accepted the story as the truth. At some point, you found out Santa Claus was really your parents and other family members. So, you stopped putting your faith in this illusion disguised as truth. In time, your Santa Claus belief no longer affected you because you no longer gave it power or attention! (Did you pass this Santa Claus story on to others? Why?)

Your Beliefs

We all carry around multitudes of beliefs. Some we know, others are operating on autopilot behind the scenes. Many that run in the background formed back in childhood or from traumatic experiences. Not all are bad or wrong, but some work against us! The most important thing to consider is what affect (positive or negative) your beliefs are having in your daily life.

The great news is . . . We don't need to relive anything to change our beliefs!

Noticing how our body feels (or emotions that surface) and determining if a particular belief requires change or release is all that is needed. We have the power to release our stress, drama, grief, and trauma by setting our intentions and doing healing practices. (Chapter Ten provides some of these practices. A future book in this series will be all about healing practices.)

My Experience

When I first began reawakening my spiritual gifts, my progress was slow. Patience was not my virtue, and I sensed there was something else slowing me down. I was right. My autopilot was running this entire set of beliefs that had brought me the same results year after year. It seemed like I was stuck on a weird merry-go-round and couldn't get off. I had a scarcity money story, low self-worth, and feared speaking up for myself. I also gave away my power of Free Will trying to please others. These beliefs drove my life experiences of always being broke, choosing the wrong people for relationships, doing what others wanted, and allowing my zest for life to come close to dying!

Using what I call "baby steps," I took each belief wreaking havoc in my life and traded it for a new one. Some were easier to change than others (like choosing better people to share my life with).

Some took longer than others (like holding myself responsible for not being able to protect my younger brother).

Am I always in balance now with all my belief-related woes solved? No, things come up from time to time. When they do, I've learned it means there's something I still need to learn (or let go of) in that area. I can say my life is <u>significantly</u> better compared to the dumpster fire it used to be.

Exercise 1: Negative Words, Thoughts, and Emotions

There are many reasons why we may use negative words or feel negative emotions. Maybe we are stressed with life and allow our emotions to get the best of us. The key is to not allow negative words, thoughts, and emotions to become a daily habit. Remember, the subconscious mind works very hard to help you create what you focus your energy and attention on!

<u>This exercise is designed to help you</u>:
Step back and take a look at how often negative words, thoughts, or emotions come up in your daily life. Sometimes we don't even realize that we've formed a negative habit! Once we can recognize what is going on, it's easier to make adjustments to our daily habits.

When you can do this exercise:
You only have to do this exercise once! (If you find yourself falling back into negative words, thoughts, or emotions, complete the exercise again.)

Time needed: 30 minutes.

What you will need:

1. A quiet, comfortable space where you can read and write.
2. Your journal and something to write with.

Reminder:
Review the entire exercise (including the notes) before completing it.

Follow these steps:

1. Sit in a comfortable position.
2. **Breathe in**. Through your nose, slowly filling your belly with air.
3. **Breathe out**. Through your mouth, slow and easy, until your belly goes flat.
4. **Repeat** 4 cycles of deep breathing.

5. **Write in your journal** any negative words, thoughts, or emotions you've had <u>about yourself</u> in the last week. Are these new or have they been around a while? (For instance, do you say things to yourself like: "I'm always broke."; "I'm stupid."; "I'm ugly."; or "I can't find a job."?)
6. **Write in your journal** any negative words, thoughts, or emotions you've had <u>about other people</u> in the last week. Write down their names. Are these individuals new to your life, or have they been around for a while? (Do any of these individuals always bring unnecessary drama? What is it about them you don't like or disagree with, etc.?)
7. Think about how your life is going right now. Write down your thoughts about it. Have your life patterns changed recently or have they been this way for some time?
8. Reflect on your current relationships with others. Are these relationships positive or negative? Are the negative relationships recent or constant with familiar individuals? (Is there a family member, co-worker, or other acquaintance you'd rather not be around?)

9. Do you see any correlation between these? Are your words, thoughts, and emotions of the last week similar to ones from the past? Do you experience any negative effects from these in your daily life?
10. Once you've completed the exercise, take a few moments to relax and do some deep breathing.

NOTE 1: After completing the practice, remember to be good to yourself and allow any emotions to come out. Eat healthy food, drink filtered water, and get plenty of rest.

NOTE 2: Be sure to write about any experiences you have over the next two days in your journal!

NOTE 3: **Wait at least 2 days before moving on to the next exercise!** This allows your body, mind, and spirit time to adjust.

Exercise 2: Your Beliefs (Part 1)

We all have a unique set of beliefs based on our learned knowledge. Some of our beliefs are good and work for us. Others work against us by opposing our inherent knowledge. It's important to figure out which ones may be causing us to create what we don't want in life.

This exercise is designed to help you:
Step back and take a look at your beliefs about yourself, others, and life. Evaluate how your life is going, and determining which beliefs may need revision or change. It is the process I used after I realized I had to change my beliefs and behaviors if I wanted my life to change. (You will need this list to complete the second part of this exercise.)

When you can do this exercise:
You only have to do this exercise once!

Time needed: 20 minutes.

What you will need:

1. A quiet, comfortable space where you can read and write.
2. A timer.
3. Your journal and something to write with.

Reminder:
Review the entire exercise (including the notes) before completing it.

Follow these steps:

1. Sit in a comfortable position.
2. **Breathe in**. Through your nose, slowly filling your belly with air.
3. **Breathe out**. Through your mouth, slow and easy, until your belly goes flat.
4. **Repeat** 4 cycles of deep breathing.
5. Write this heading in your journal: "I Believe This About . . . "
6. Write these categories in columns across the pages: Myself, Others, Money, My Health, Relationships, Religion, Spirituality, My Family, and The World.
7. Set a timer for 20 minutes.
8. When you're ready, start the timer. List all the beliefs/thoughts that come to mind about each category. (You're just emptying your thoughts onto paper. Don't try to analyze them.)
9. Once you've written all the beliefs that came to mind, you're done! (If other beliefs pop into your head later on, write them down as well.)
10. Once you've completed the exercise, take a few moments to relax and do some deep breathing.

NOTE 1: After completing the practice, remember to be good to yourself and allow any emotions to come out. Eat healthy food, drink filtered water and get plenty of rest.

NOTE 2: Be sure to write about any experiences you have over the next two days in your journal!

NOTE 3: **Wait at least 2 days before going on to the next exercise!** This is to allow time for your body, mind, and spirit to adjust.

Exercise 2: Your Beliefs (Part 2)

When you can do this exercise:
You only have to do this exercise once!

Time needed: 30 minutes.

What you will need:

1. A quiet, comfortable space where you can read and write.
2. A timer.
3. Your journal and something to write with.
4. The "I Believe This About . . . " list from Part One.

Reminder:
Review the entire exercise (including the notes) before completing it.

Follow these steps:

1. Sit in a comfortable position.
2. **Breathe in**. Through your nose, slowly filling your belly with air.
3. **Breathe out**. Through your mouth, slow and easy, until your belly goes flat.
4. **Repeat** 4 cycles of deep breathing.
5. Set a timer for 30 minutes.
6. For each belief you listed in Part 1, ask: Where did I learn/accept this belief? (From whom? Where? When? Why?) You don't have to recall all the details.
7. For each belief you listed in Part 1, ask: Is this belief affecting my life in a positive or negative way?
8. For each belief you listed in Part 1, ask: Knowing what I do now, do I still have faith this belief is serving me well? (Circle the ones you no longer believe have a positive effect on your life.)
9. Once you've completed the exercise, take a few moments to relax and do some deep breathing.

NOTE 1: After completing the practice, remember to be good to yourself and allow any emotions to come out. Eat healthy, drink filtered water, and get plenty of rest.

NOTE 2: Be sure to write about any experiences you have over the next two days in your journal!

NOTE 3: **Wait at least 2 days before going on to the next exercise!** This will allow your body, mind, and spirit time to adjust.

Exercise: Comparing Your Beliefs to Spiritual Truths

Once we've written down (and thought about) our beliefs, we can compare them to the spiritual truths we covered in Chapter Seven. Think of the spiritual truths in Chapter Seven as the magnifying glass we use to clearly see the positive or negative effects of our beliefs.

This exercise is designed to help you:
Determine which beliefs may not be in alignment with spiritual truth. In other words, you will be able to see which beliefs are working against you versus for you. This will reveal beliefs that may be causing undesirable, repeating patterns in your life.

<u>When you can do this exercise</u>:
You only have to do this exercise once!

<u>Time needed</u>: 20 minutes.

<u>What you will need</u>:

1. A quiet, comfortable space to read and write.
2. Your journal, something to write with, and a highlighter or colored pen.
3. List of spiritual truths from Chapter 7.
4. List of your beliefs from Exercise 2, Part 1.

<u>Reminder</u>:
Review the entire practice (including the notes) before completing it.

<u>Follow these steps</u>:

1. Sit in a comfortable position.
2. **Breathe in**. Through your nose, slowly filling your belly with air.
3. **Breathe out**. Through your mouth, slow and easy, until your belly goes flat.
4. **Repeat** 4 cycles of deep breathing.
5. **Review** the spiritual truths from Chapter 7.

6. Look at each of the beliefs you listed in Exercise 2, Part 1. **Highlight** any belief that isn't in alignment with any of the spiritual truths listed in Chapter 7.
7. Go back over your belief list again and **circle** any beliefs you know are causing stress, drama, grief, trauma, or other negatives in your life.
8. Review your list once more and **make an "X"** next to any beliefs that seem outdated, not yours, aren't historically a positive influence on your life, or prevent you from being true to yourself and your beliefs. (Ex: Santa Claus, penance, money is evil, etc.)
9. Once you've completed the exercise, take a few moments to relax and do some deep breathing.

NOTE 1: This exercise is not to tell you if your beliefs are positive or negative. It allows you to look at them and decide which ones are no longer serving you or causing difficulties in your life.

NOTE 2: The law of Free Will is always in effect! This means you choose whether you want to keep, revise, or change any of your beliefs.

NOTE 3: If you need help to decide about your beliefs, just take some deep breaths and ask for help.

WHAT DO YOU BELIEVE? 117

If the belief feels good in your body (aligned with your Source OS), it's a "keeper". If you feel tension, pain, or hesitation in your body (not aligned with your Source OS or the spiritual truths), consider changing it.

NOTE 4: After completing the exercise, remember to be good to yourself and allow any emotions to come out. Eat healthy food, drink filtered water, and get plenty of rest.

NOTE 5: Be sure to write about any experiences you have over the next two days in your journal!

NOTE 6: **Wait at least 2 days before going on to the next exercise!** This is to allow time for your body, mind, and spirit to adjust.

In this chapter, we took a deep dive into our beliefs and discovered those we need to change (based on whether they are bringing positive or negative into our lives). We learned how to determine if our beliefs align with spiritual truths and our Source OS. The most difficult step in solving any problem is recognizing when there is a problem and what the problem is. Once you've determined the problem, it's a simple matter of solving the problem. But how do we solve the "problem" of having beliefs that aren't serving our Highest Good?

9
Changing Old Beliefs

*Things of the past must remain in the past.
It is where they belong.*

Up to this point, we have discovered our Source OS and have a basic understanding of spiritual truths. We've also identified some beliefs that aren't acting as a positive force in our lives. In this chapter, we'll uncover the beliefs responsible for the repeating negative cycles in our life. We'll also develop the skills to transform those negative beliefs into positive ones.

We carry around an entire book of beliefs based on our life experiences. Almost all of them we formed back in childhood. Beliefs are the things we agreed to (and accepted as truth) back when we had a child's mind. We adopted these beliefs and took them into adulthood with us, not yet knowing how they would affect our lives.

It is important to remember that every belief and every experience is a teacher. Some people or experiences taught us good or helpful lessons. From others, we learned harsh lessons that were not (and still are not) helpful or healthful for us. Again, this is not to place blame. It is to help us understand these teachers were using what they learned, experienced, and accepted as truth. Like us, many of them were unaware of their inherent knowledge and lived their whole lives operating from just their learned knowledge. They passed their learned knowledge (however good or bad it may have been) on to us.

When we become adults and handle our own choices, we can use our Free Will to change or create whatever we choose. Some changes are simple (like living or working in a different city). Other changes (like beliefs) require more work. Having learned to rely on our knowledge mind and ignore our spiritual, we have a little more expanding to do. That expanding includes waking up and using our Source OS. You don't have to build it from scratch!

On Changing Learned Knowledge or Beliefs

Some beliefs will resist being changed. Especially the beliefs we have about ourselves and the world based on some type of abuse, bullying, racism, prejudice, religious teachings, etc. Know that it's okay! We can live a better life by choosing the positive we came here with and releasing anything that doesn't serve our Highest Good! Our goal is to balance our Source OS with the aspects of our learned knowledge that support a happy and prosperous life.

We can work on changing a belief several times a day. Which activities and times work best will depend on each person. I suggest using as many activities as possible. When we first start out, the more energy, imagery, and feeling we put into changing a belief, the quicker we'll see results. This means doing it several times a day. It's not time-consuming, so it should be easy. (The exercises at the chapter's end describe these activities and recommended times.) Now that we have a deeper understanding of beliefs and the effort involved in altering them, there are four immediate steps you can take to get the most from this chapter:

1. Be willing to release any old or false beliefs you've held.
2. Be willing to receive guidance in your preferred way.
3. Trust you will know which beliefs to change, and how you'll revise or create new ones.
4. Agree to take it easy on yourself and work in baby steps. (It took time for you to create your beliefs. It will take time to change or improve them.)

The best part of changing false or negative beliefs (besides being happier and more balanced) is that each change has a cascading affect on other beliefs. This means the changed belief alters any related beliefs by changing or reducing the strength of those beliefs. You may observe this cascade after changing your first belief. When returning to your belief list to choose another belief to change, you'll notice the remaining beliefs don't seem as overwhelming as when you first wrote them. You may discover one or more beliefs on your list you no longer believe and/or you're no longer experiencing in your life!

This cascade affect happens once we recognize The Truth (inherent knowledge) and choose it over beliefs that contradict our inherent knowledge.

Anything not aligned with our inherent knowledge or Source OS will fall away. It falls away because we no longer give it the power it needs to thrive!

My Experience

For me, releasing/changing old beliefs was scary at first. The task seemed overwhelming because my list of beliefs to change was long. I thought it would be difficult and take forever! I took it slow, treated myself with patience and love, and never gave up. Giving up meant going back to the life of misery I was trying to leave forever!

The way I tackled my list was to pick **one** false belief that seemed easy to change and start there. As I experienced success, I started using my intuition to choose the next belief to change. I would review my list, and as I read each old belief, a remaining one would stand out for me to take on next. The first belief I changed was the belief it would be hard and take a long time. Sounds simple, but it was essential for me to begin my belief makeover. It's amazing how changing your mind about something makes it easier to accomplish!

First, I wrote my belief releasing statement, "I am releasing any beliefs that no longer serve my Highest Good with ease and grace." Then I would say, feel, and visualize my statement multiple times during the day.

Changing my first belief was hard (and seemed to take a long time), but each belief after that was easier to change! Frequently, I would look at my old beliefs list and realize I no longer believed one or two on the list!

The act of changing my mindset and one belief had weakened or changed others! This is a great example of the exponential (cascading) affect that changing beliefs have on other beliefs. What is at work here is the law or principle of truth being constant and lies falling away in the light of The Truth. Once we discover and recognize The Truth, all the falsehoods fall away from us.

Have I released all my negative beliefs? No, I know events happen in our lives and we form new beliefs out of those experiences. The worldwide crisis that began in 2020 is one example. The world had not experienced anything like this event in recent memory. We had to make quick decisions to protect ourselves and our family. All of us had our eyes opened to what was most important in life during that time. Perhaps now is a good time to review any beliefs we formed during this event and determine if they pass The Truth test.

(An "Ah-ha!" moment I had while writing this chapter was I still have one belief from childhood that needs more attention as it is affecting my physical. Perhaps it's been hiding way back in my subconscious somewhere, but it's become obvious that it is next on my list.

For those who have read my memoir, you can probably guess what I'm talking about. Maybe it will be a topic I write about in the future.)

Releasing Old Beliefs Exercises

In previous chapters, we discussed our subconscious mind and what we think, say, do, and feel. We're going to use those same tools to change the beliefs that are no longer a positive influence on our lives. Since the subconscious focuses on bringing into our lives those things we give our energy and attention to, we will change what we give our time and energy to. We are reinforcing our new beliefs through think, say, do, and feel!

In this series of exercises you will:

1. Choose one old belief you want to change right now.
2. Write your new belief that will replace the old one.
3. Release the old belief by disagreement.
4. State and agree with your new belief.
5. Reinforce your new belief throughout the day until you experience sustained results in your life.

You are creating a practice designed to reprogram (or refocus) your subconscious mind (telling it what you want now). Make sure you set aside quiet, undisturbed time to complete the exercises. Complete exercises 1-4 back-to-back. Read each exercise (and any notes) before you complete it. Write your answers and experiences in your journal!

Exercise 1: Choose Your Old Belief

<u>This exercise is designed to help you</u>:
Choose one belief you want to change from your belief list.

<u>When you can do this exercise</u>:
Do this practice each time you are ready to select a belief to change.

<u>Time needed</u>: 15 minutes.

<u>What you will need</u>:

1. A quiet, comfortable space to read and write.
2. Your highlighted belief list from Chapter 8.
3. Your journal and something to write with.

Reminder:
Review the entire exercise (including the notes) before completing it.

Follow these steps:

1. Sit in a comfortable position.
2. **Breathe in.** Through your nose, slowly filling your belly with air.
3. **Breathe out.** Through your mouth, slow and easy, until your belly goes flat.
4. **Repeat** 4 cycles of deep breathing.
5. **Review** your highlighted belief list from Chapter 8.
6. **Choose** one negative you said about yourself, or one belief that contradicts spiritual truths, that you'd like most to change right now. (Trust any gut feeling or intuition you receive.)
7. On a new page in your journal **write**, "Old Belief" and put the belief you selected next to it.
8. **Give thanks** to the old belief for whatever it taught you or how it helped you in the past. (Write your thanks in your journal! Be generic if you can't think of specifics.)
9. **Quiet your mind** (take a few deep breaths) and decide to change this one belief.

10. **Breathe out** and state aloud, "I am willing to release any belief that no longer serves my Highest Good."
11. **Breathe in** and say aloud, "I am."
12. Once you've completed the exercise, take a few moments to relax and do some deep breathing.

Example:
Old belief: "There's never enough money."

Give thanks: Thank you for showing me the negative effects this belief had on my life. It taught me to take actions that ensured my poverty. (List some lessons you've learned from it.) I understand what I've experienced until now was the best outcome for this belief (or something similar).

Intention statement: "I am willing to release any belief that no longer serves my Highest Good. I am."

NOTE 1: Some behaviors have a connection to another, deeper belief. Don't worry about connecting the dots right away. The connection will reveal itself in time. An example of a deeper, connected belief is someone who eats, smokes, drinks, or uses drugs to cope with life. They want to stop these behaviors, but the root belief behind their behaviors may be trauma.

Once they address the trauma, releasing the behaviors completely will be a lot easier and last long-term.

NOTE 2: The words "any belief" proclaims your willingness to release not only the belief you chose, but any related beliefs!

Exercise 2: Write Your New Belief

<u>This exercise is designed to help you</u>:
Create a new belief to replace your old belief.

<u>When you can do this exercise</u>:
Do this exercise (along with Exercise 1) each time you change one of your beliefs.

<u>Time needed</u>: 15 minutes.

<u>What you will need</u>:

1. A quiet, comfortable space to read and write.
2. Your journal and something to write with.

<u>Reminder</u>:
Review the entire exercise (including the notes) before completing it.

Follow these steps:

1. Sit in a comfortable position.
2. **Breathe in**. Through your nose, slowly filling your belly with air.
3. **Breathe out**. Through your mouth, slow and easy, until your belly goes flat.
4. **Repeat** 4 cycles of deep breathing.
5. Look at the old belief you wrote about in your journal.
6. **Create** a new belief that replaces the old one. Do this by turning it into a positive belief that is for your Highest Good. Use this template: "I am ___. I am."
7. **Write**, "My New Belief" on your journal page, then write your new belief next to it.
8. Once you've completed the exercise, take a few moments to relax and do some deep breathing.

Example 1:

Old belief: "I'm fat and out of shape."
New belief: "I am perfect health. I am." OR "I am choosing healthy food and exercise. I am."

Example 2:

Old belief: "I'm always broke."
New belief: "I am making good money decisions. I am."
OR "I am prosperous/abundant. I am."

NOTE 1: Write your new belief in your own words, but keep it short and positive.

NOTE 2: Avoid using "not," "going to," or "will." Remember, everything that follows "I am." must be positive and in the present tense!

Exercise 3: Release Your Old Belief

This exercise is designed to help you:
Release your old belief by disagreeing with it (not believing in it anymore). You agreed to it (and adopted it) at some moment in the past. Now you're going to disagree with it because you no longer want ownership of it AND it isn't serving your Highest Good or your Divine Self.

When you can do this exercise:
Do this exercise (along with Exercise 1 and 2) each time you change one of your beliefs.

<u>Time needed</u>: 15 minutes.

<u>What you will need</u>:

1. A quiet, comfortable space to read and write.
2. The old belief you chose from Exercise 1.
3. Your journal and something to write with.

<u>Reminder</u>:
Review the entire exercise (including the notes) before completing it.

<u>Follow these steps</u>:

1. Sit in a comfortable position.
2. **Breathe in**. Through your nose, slowly filling your belly with air.
3. **Breathe out**. Through your mouth, slow and easy, until your belly goes flat.
4. **Repeat** 4 cycles of deep breathing.
5. Look at the old belief you chose from Exercise 1.
6. **Write** your disagreement on your journal page using this template: "I no longer believe _____. I am releasing this belief in its entirety now. I am."

7. Once you've written your disagreement and releasing statement, take a few deep breaths to relax, then **say it aloud** three times.
8. After you've stated your disagreement three times, state, "It is said. It is so."
9. Once you've released the old belief, go back to your journal and draw a line or "X" through your old belief. It is no longer a part of your life! (You won't give it any more of your energy or attention.)
10. Once you've completed the exercise, take a few moments to relax and do some deep breathing.

Example:

Old belief: "I'm fat and out of shape."
Disagreement: "I no longer believe I have to be fat and out of shape. I am releasing this belief in its entirety now. I am. It is said. It is so."

Exercise 4: State Your New Belief

This exercise is designed to help you:
Replace your old belief (you released in the previous exercise) with your new belief.

(This new belief is the one you will give your energy and attention to starting immediately.)

<u>When you can do this exercise</u>:
Do this exercise (along with exercises 1-3) each time you change one of your beliefs.

<u>Time needed</u>: 15 minutes.

<u>What you will need</u>:

1. A quiet, comfortable space to read and write.
2. The new belief you wrote in Exercise 2.
3. Your journal and something to write with.

<u>Reminder</u>:
Review the entire exercise (including the notes) before completing it.

<u>Follow these steps</u>:

1. Sit in a comfortable position.
2. **Breathe in.** Through your nose, slowly filling your belly with air.
3. **Breathe out.** Through your mouth, slow and easy, until your belly goes flat.
4. **Repeat** 4 cycles of deep breathing.

5. **Review** your new belief (from Exercise 2). Make sure it is positive, written in present tense, and reflects what you are choosing to believe now.
6. **Breathe out** and say your new belief aloud: "I am ____."
7. **Breathe in** and say: "I am."
8. **State**: "It is said. It is so."
9. Close your eyes and imagine how it feels to have this new belief. Imagine the positive changes you will experience in your life because of this new belief.
10. Once you've finished, go back to your journal page and write, "This is me!" below your new belief statement. Put a big circle around both with a highlighter or colored ink pen (except red). Draw a smiley face or put happy stickers on it. Celebrate! (Your new belief is the one you'll be focusing your thoughts, words, actions, and feelings on until it becomes automatic in your life.)

Example:

Breathe out and say aloud: "I am choosing healthy food and exercise."
Breathe in and say: "I am."
State: "It is said. It is so."

Imagine: Looking in the mirror and liking what you see! Feeling more energetic and happy! Buying new clothes in smaller sizes! Your body becoming more toned and your skin vibrant and healthy!

NOTE: If you feel resistance or phony when saying your positive belief statement, it's just your old habit (learned knowledge) talking. Remember, the subconscious doesn't know truth from fiction!

Exercise 5: Reinforcing Your New Belief

<u>This exercise is designed to help you</u>:
Experience and reinforce your new belief several times a day so it will quickly (and more easily) become a part of you. This is important to creating new habits that will positively affect your daily life.

Releasing old beliefs (and adopting new ones) is spiritual work. Remember, we learn spiritual practices by doing (experiencing). This means we think, say, do, and feel our new beliefs! We pay no attention to what was (old belief) because we placed it in the past where it belongs.

<u>When you can do this exercise</u>:
Do these practices every time you change one of your beliefs.

CHANGING OLD BELIEFS 137

<u>Time needed</u>: 5 minutes.

<u>What you will need</u>:

1. Short blocks of time during the day to reinforce your new belief.
2. The new belief you stated from Exercise 4.
3. Your journal and something to write with.

Everyone can find five extra minutes here and there during their day to reinforce their new belief. For example:

1. Before you go to sleep. (This is the <u>minimum</u> you must do! Refer to Exercise 6.)
2. In the morning, when you wake up. (If you need to wake up a few minutes earlier, do it. Go to bed a few minutes earlier.)
3. Anytime it comes to mind during the day. (On work breaks, lunchtime, or whenever you have a few extra minutes to spare.)
4. As part of your daily relax/wind-down time. (If you aren't giving yourself this break every day, you need to start.)
5. Whenever you want to ask (or give thanks) for any help you've received.

Reminder:
Review the exercise (including the notes) before completing it.

Follow these steps:

1. Sit in a comfortable position.
2. **Breathe in.** Through your nose, slowly filling your belly with air.
3. **Breathe out.** Through your mouth, slow and easy, until your belly goes flat.
4. **Repeat** 4 cycles of deep breathing.
5. **Breathe out** and say your new belief aloud (unless you're somewhere you don't want others to hear): "I am _____." It is important to hear it in your own voice (see Note 7).
6. **Breathe in** and say: "I am."
7. **Close your eyes** and see yourself living that belief. Can you envision how your life will improve with this new belief? Ask, "How does it feel to already BE living that belief?" Do you feel happier, content, energized, or calm? Allow yourself to FEEL how it feels.
8. Continue to say your new belief while seeing and feeling how your life is improving for a few more breaths (or minutes).

CHANGING OLD BELIEFS

Example:

Let's use the "I am choosing healthy food and exercise. I am." belief from Exercise 2.

1. State the new belief aloud while . . .
2. Visualizing yourself eating healthy food, losing weight, drinking water, going to the gym or walking, and buying new (smaller-sized) clothes. See how good you look in the mirror! See the smile on your face!
3. As you're seeing yourself . . . also feel how it feels as your new belief brings about these things in your life. Feel the happiness, energy, and vitality that come from being healthy!

NOTE 1: Everyone will have their own unique way of seeing and feeling their new belief. Use your imagination to create a realistic mini-movie in your mind. It should have vibrant colors and sounds, you as the star, and bring about positive feelings when you watch it!

NOTE 2: What you are doing is putting intent, a vision, and feelings into your subconscious. You're instructing your subconscious, "This is what I want!" You are reinforcing this is who you are now (not who I am becoming, but who I am).

NOTE 3: Every time you do your practice, you are investing more time and intent into what you are creating in your life! (For example, when you do your practice before sleep, your subconscious has about eight hours to work on it! Multiply eight hours times seven days and that's 56 hours a week or 240 hours a month of solid work while you sleep!)

NOTE 4: When you released your old belief, you let go of the past associated with it. Allow the past to stay in the past. If the past comes up again, ask what more you can learn from it. Thank the past for the lesson, then let it go. You can let it go by stating, "I am releasing any past that no longer serves my Highest Good. I am."

NOTE 5: Some negative words, thoughts, emotions, and actions about yourself are old and may take longer to change into positives. Keep practicing until your negative has changed. Find things that reinforce your new truth about yourself. (Refer to the chapter on spiritual truths.)

NOTE 6: It may seem overwhelming to change a belief or habit. Changing beliefs (creating something new) isn't supposed to be difficult! Spiritual learning is supposed to be easy so <u>anyone</u> can do it. It's designed that way. People complicate it because of our learned knowledge and not being familiar with our spiritual selves.

Changing a belief is as simple as deciding to believe something else and not giving the old belief another thought or moment of your time/energy. In other words, we can simply change our mind about anything! (We did this in Exercise 3.)

NOTE 7: You can make your belief practice more powerful by creating a voice recording that includes your new belief statement, how the new belief feels, and what you see in life with your new belief. (Do you feel happier, content, energized, or calm? Do you see yourself smiling more, exercising, having fun, or looking healthy?) Use your imagination to create a realistic narrative of how your new belief will play out.

Example:

Record your new belief: "I am choosing healthy food and exercise. I am."

Record how it will feel: "I am having fun on my walks and when I go to the gym. I feel more in control of my body and life. I feel stronger and have more energy."

Record what you will see: "I notice I'm smiling more and friends have commented on how happy I seem. When I look in the mirror, I can tell my body is more toned.

I am eating a variety of colorful fruits and vegetables and feel more vibrant and energetic."

NOTE 1: Your new belief recording will be longer and much more detailed than this example. (This example is to show you how to get started.)

NOTE 2: Use a positive tone of voice when you record your narrative. Once it's recorded, listen to it throughout the day with earbuds or headphones. You can listen in your car on the way to work, on the bus or train (if safe), while cooking dinner, while relaxing after work, or before you fall asleep at night.

So, as we repeat aloud our new belief, we also imagine how we look and feel with this new belief! Don't allow any contradictory daily life experiences to discourage you! The more you practice, the more your daily life experiences will change!

Exercise 6: Reinforcing Before Sleep Sequence

<u>This exercise is designed to help you</u>:
Reinforce your new belief and tell your subconscious what you really want to experience in your life.

<u>When you can do this exercise</u>:
Do this every night before sleep for every belief you change.

<u>Time needed</u>: 5 minutes.

<u>What you will need</u>:

1. A quiet, comfortable space to sleep.
2. Your new belief (or your belief voice recording from Exercise 5, Note 7). If you prefer to listen to your voice recording as you're going to sleep (versus simply saying and imagining your new belief), you'll need to record it on an "old school" type device. (No smart phones or other electronic devices in your bedroom!)

<u>Reminder</u>:
Review the entire exercise (including the notes) before completing it.

<u>Follow these steps</u>:

1. Prepare for sleep and lay in a comfortable sleeping position.
2. **Breathe in**. Through your nose, slowly filling your belly with air.

3. **Breathe out.** Through your mouth, slow and easy, until your belly goes flat.
4. **Repeat** 4 cycles of deep breathing.
5. **Breathe out and say** your new belief, "I am _____." (Or start your voice recording here.)
6. **Breathe in and say,** "I am."
7. **Close your eyes** and see yourself living that belief. Envision how your life will improve with this new belief. How does it feel to BE that belief? Do you feel happier, content, energized, or calm? Allow yourself to FEEL how it feels.
8. Continue to say your new belief while seeing and feeling how your life is improving until you fall asleep. (Or listen to your voice narration as you fall asleep.)

Example:

Let's use the new belief: "I am choosing healthy food and exercise. I am."

1. Do four cycles of deep breathing.
2. Breathe out and state, "I am choosing healthy food and exercise."
3. Breathe in and state, "I am."

CHANGING OLD BELIEFS

4. Continue stating your belief in this way while seeing and feeling the results your new belief is having on your life.
5. Continue until you fall asleep!
6. After you wake up, journal about any experiences or changes you notice in your mood, sleep, energy, dreams, or other.

NOTE 1: As you reinforce your new belief, you may feel weird, get emotional for no reason, or want more sleep. You may question more beliefs or decide not to believe things you used to. There's no cause for alarm! It is releasing the old so the new can come in!

NOTE 2: Let whatever wants to come out do so! You'll feel much better! Treat yourself well. Get plenty of rest. Eat nutritious food and drink plenty of spring or filtered water (no tap or drinking water).
Journal any thoughts, experiences, insights, emotions, or other you may have.

NOTE 3: You will live life as if you've already adopted your new belief! Stop and ask for help to make sure new decisions are based upon your new belief and spiritual truths.

NOTE 4: Recommend removing all electronics from your sleeping space. Having electronics in your bedroom interrupts your sleep cycle! (See Chapter 11 for a brief overview.)

In this chapter, we've looked at our beliefs and decided which ones we want to change. We learned how to release an old belief, write a new belief, and reinforce the new belief until it becomes part of who we are. Once you've adopted your first new belief, repeat the process to change the next belief on your belief list! Keep changing the beliefs on your list until you've crossed them all off.

As you go back to your original belief list, notice any beliefs that don't exist anymore. Journal about any remaining beliefs that aren't as strong as before. Such is the power of the cascading or exponential affect of adopting new beliefs. As you take on new beliefs, it's helpful to do other types of healing or releasing to make adopting your new belief easier. **Wait at least a week** after you begin reinforcing your new belief, then follow me to the next chapter on healing practices . . .

10

Releasing Grief, Stress, Anger, and More (Healing Practices)

Unreleased negative will find a way out through physical, spiritual, or psychological disease.

Our body, mind, and spirit adjust to the inherent knowledge we're exploring, and when we change what we think, say, do, and feel. In this chapter, we will experience healing practices to add to our growing list of newfound spiritual skills and abilities. These practices help our body release various forms of negative energy, maintain balance, stay grounded, and regain energy.

Rest and rejuvenation are essential for our body, mind, and spirit to perform at its optimum. We often work eight hours a day, five days a week, have long commutes, and complete daily tasks before and after work.

We catch up on other tasks over the weekend, like cleaning our living space, doing yard work, and washing all the clothes that piled up during the week. Often, we also have a "to do" list that is never finished. As we cross off one task, we find another to add to the list. At bedtime, exhaustion and stress prevent us from sleeping or sleeping well.

Is it any wonder we're constantly tired, feel irritable, or are simply not enjoying life like we should? When we start our spiritual work of adopting new beliefs, the body and mind will align with our new beliefs. What we are thinking, saying, doing, and feeling throughout the day will also adjust. During this time, unresolved negative thoughts or emotions connected to old beliefs will adjust. We cannot change beliefs without also removing any imbalance associated with said beliefs.

Something (or someone) caused our beliefs to form. Perhaps we were teased and laughed at by kids at school for being heavier than others. Over time, this caused hurt feelings and low self-esteem. Maybe we endured years of name-calling. As an adult, we aren't overweight, but we still believe our bodies are somehow flawed. Hurtful words from classmates (and how their words made us feel) remain in our subconscious until we release them!

As we make changes, we need to honor whatever comes up and allow it to release in its natural way. How much stuff is waiting to be released is different for everyone. Releasing what we've been holding inside will happen at our own speed and time. When we decide to release any negative we've been holding inside, it always releases in measured amounts. What this means is, the amount of negative released will be exactly what is needed at that particular time.

What is this stuff that needs releasing? It is feelings and emotions from past negative experiences that are causing negative results in our daily lives. They are the emotions and feelings we neglected to release when they needed to be released. The past may be recent past or long past (childhood). We are unaware of a lot of these unreleased feelings and emotions. Some we are aware of and choose to ignore or try our best to forget them.

Our body and mind will attempt to balance themselves with our new beliefs. Allow any feelings and emotions to express themselves unrestricted. What this means is if (for known or unknown reasons) you feel like crying, cry. If you get angry, punch a pillow, scream in private, or workout at the gym. Knowing why it's happening, or reliving anything, is not important. Simply allow for the safe release of whatever your body, mind, or spirit needs to release.

We can also assist our body, mind, and spirit by doing practices to reduce or remove built-up stress, grief, trauma, or other negative. The practices in this chapter will aid us in accomplishing that. Learn to use them now and then make them a permanent part of daily life. They will assist in maintaining lower levels of stress, increase energy levels, and enhance a sense of overall well-being.

My Experience

I received the news of my grandfather's death when I was a junior in high school. A little over a month later, my grandma also died. During this time, my living situation was filled with stress, drama, abuse, and neglect. Holding myself together was all I could manage on a normal day. My survival mode kicked in, and I became numb to the feelings and emotions associated with the deaths of people I treasured most in life. Grieving for my grandparents was just too overwhelming for me to handle.

After some time, I escaped my horrible living situation. I started missing my grandparents and the farm where I had created so many fond childhood memories. As my longing for the good 'ol days intensified, I would burst into tears for what I thought was no reason. I thought my crying was because I was feeling miserable in my life.

One day (out of the blue), I felt an overwhelming need to return to my grandparent's farm. The only place where I'd felt alive and free during my childhood. The past was pulling me back. I didn't understand what was happening to me. I just knew I had to go, and nothing would stop me. It felt as if an external force was compelling me to go.

Even though it had been years since my last visit, I remembered the exact route. All the trees that once lined the familiar gravel road were gone. As the old homestead came into view, I witnessed the log cabin and barn reduced to piles of rubble. The gardens and orchard had returned to the earth. All my memories of my place of refuge were gone. At that moment, the full weight of the loss of my grandparents hit me. I fell to my knees and cried, asking God, "Why?" as I wailed.

The grief I had held inside all those years was released. My spirit had urged me to go back so I could grieve. That day, I released an unbelievable grief that was necessary for healing. Had I kept all that grief bottled up inside, who knows how it would have affected my life? That experience taught me that releasing emotions is a gift. Grieving removes an enormous weight from our body, mind, and spirit. When we grieve, we are healing and cleansing.

Healing/Releasing Practices

Doing these practices will help make changing your beliefs easier. Read over each exercise before completing it. Journal your experiences while completing these practices. Connecting with nature, sunlight, and fresh air all play a part in the effectiveness of these exercises.

The crystals/stones and essential oils recommended for each practice are optional. They are used to increase the effectiveness of the practice. (Note: Please do a skin test before using any essential oil to make sure you don't have a reaction.)

Practice: Stress Buster Breathing

Stress Buster Breathing is a foundational practice we can use throughout the day to relieve stress and calm ourselves. We started using it in the third chapter, but I'm including it here, so all the essential practices will be in one place. The effects of the practice will be more powerful if done outside in nature!

<u>This practice is designed to help you</u>:
Reduce your stress level, bring a sense of calm and balance, increase your oxygen intake, and clear your head.

Most of us don't get enough oxygen! We need to practice breathing deeply!

<u>When you can do this practice</u>:
You can do this practice anytime . . . anywhere! Stressed at work? Take a couple of minutes to do this exercise! Stuck in rush-hour traffic? Do this simple practice and feel the stress melt away! Finally make it home after a long day? Complete the practice outside!

<u>Time needed</u>: 5 minutes.

<u>What you will need</u>:

1. A quiet, comfortable space outside (preferred).
2. Something comfortable to sit or lay on.
3. <u>Essential Oil</u>: Lavender-1 to 2 drops (optional). (Lavender works to relieve stress and calm the mind.)
4. Your journal and something to write with.

<u>Reminder</u>:
Review the entire practice (including the notes) before completing it.

Follow these steps:

1. Sit or lay in a comfortable position.
2. **Apply**: 1 drop of Lavender essential oil onto your skin and inhale the scent (optional).
3. Close your eyes (optional).
4. **Breathe in**. Through your nose, slowly filling your belly with air.
5. **Breathe out**. Through your mouth, slow and easy, until your belly goes flat.
6. **Repeat** 4 cycles of deep breathing.
7. **Breathe in and visualize**: Imagine breathing in white light and it slowly filling your entire body from head to toe.
8. **Breathe out and visualize**: Imagine breathing out any negativity that may be in your body. (Do you notice any color to your exhaled breath?)
9. **Breathe in and visualize**: Continue to fill your body from head to toe with white light.
10. **Breathe out and visualize**: Continue to exhale any negative that may be in your body.
11. **Continue cycles** of breathing in white light (and exhaling any negative) until your entire body is filled with white light (and you sense there's no more negative to release).

RELEASING GRIEF, STRESS, ANGER, AND MORE

<u>Tip</u>: You can say to yourself, "I am filling my entire body with white light" as you breathe in. You can also say to yourself, "I am releasing any negative stored in my body" as you breath out. This will help you focus.

NOTE 1: Focus on your breathing and imagery. Allow random thoughts to pass.

NOTE 2: You can also imagine your exhaled air floating up into the sky to be transmuted.

NOTE 3: Never assume you have sickness or negative in your body! Simply allow any negative that <u>may</u> be there to be released.

NOTE 4: Breathing in white light is healing, energizing, and cleansing. Exhaling negative is a release and detox. Don't worry if you can't imagine white light or see a color for any negative you may have in your body! Just use the statements in the "Tip" as you do the practice.

NOTE 5: Use this practice as your daily de-stress break! Turn on some relaxing music, light a candle, burn some incense, or do whatever puts you in a relaxed mood. Then take 15 minutes and enjoy!

NOTE 6: Most of us breathe too shallow. Do more deep breathing during the day. You will feel more relaxed, reduce your stress, and give your body the oxygen it needs!

NOTE 7: Be sure to write about any experiences in your journal!

Practice: Negative Energy Release

In this practice, we are asking for help from the Earth to receive and transmute any negative we send. We are also setting our intent to release whatever stuff we've been carrying around. If we've been carrying a lot on our shoulders, or we feel like we're holding so much inside that we just might burst, this practice will help relieve that burden.

<u>This practice is designed to help you</u>:
Release any negative from your body. (This practice works best when done outdoors.)
In this practice, you will release all the "stuff" you've been holding inside. This will reduce your stress and anxiety levels, calm you, and lift the weight of life from your shoulders.

RELEASING GRIEF, STRESS, ANGER, AND MORE

<u>When you can do this practice</u>:
Do this practice anytime you feel stress and negativity building up in your body.

<u>Time needed</u>: 15 minutes.

<u>What you will need</u>:

1. A quiet, comfortable space outdoors. (The effects of the practice will be more powerful if done outside in nature!)
2. A comfortable spot of ground to stand on with your bare feet. (Use a blanket to cushion if needed.)
3. <u>Essential Oil</u>: Spikenard (optional). (Spikenard is grounding, calming, and relaxing. It is also effective for insomnia, nervousness, and anxiety. It resonates and helps balance the root chakra.)
4. <u>Crystal or Stone</u>: Red Jasper (optional). (Red Jasper helps in maintaining stability in emotions and feelings. It also helps you face hard times in your life and deal with them carefully. It will create a resonating vibration in the sacral, root, and earth chakras.)
5. Your journal and something to write with.

Reminder:
Review the entire practice (including the notes) before completing it.

Follow these steps:

1. Stand barefoot on the ground.
2. **Say**: "Mother Earth, I ask that you help me release any negative or stress stored in my body. Thank you!"
3. **Apply** 1 drop of Spikenard essential oil onto your skin and/or inhale the scent (optional).
4. **Hold** the Red Jasper stone in your non-writing hand (optional).
5. **Say**: "I am releasing any negative or stress that may be stored in my body."
6. Close your eyes.
7. **Breathe in**. Through your nose, slowly filling your belly with air.
8. **Breathe out**. Through your mouth, slow and easy, until your belly goes flat.
9. **Repeat** 4 cycles of deep breathing.
10. **Say**: "Show me the color of any stress or negative that may be stored in my body. Thank you."

RELEASING GRIEF, STRESS, ANGER, AND MORE

11. **Continue deep breathing** until you sense a color that represents any negative you may have in your body. What color is it? (If you don't sense a color, pick a <u>very</u> light grey.)
12. **Breathe out and visualize**: Imagine the color turning into a liquid.
13. **Breathe in.**
14. **Breathe out and visualize**: The colored liquid beginning to drain from your body starting at your head. Look down and see the liquid soaking into the ground through the soles of your feet.
15. **Breathe in and visualize**: Breathing in white light and it beginning to fill your body starting with your head.
16. **Breathe out and visualize**: More of the colored liquid draining from your body and soaking into the ground.
17. **Breathe in and visualize**: Breathing in white light and it filling more of your body.
18. **Continue cycles** of breathing, filling your body with white light and draining all the colored liquid from your body, until your entire body is filled with white light and all the colored liquid has drained from your body. (This may take a few minutes. Everyone is different.)

NOTE 1: If you're not able to stand for 10-15 minutes, use a chair, stool, wheelchair, or other to sit.

NOTE 2: When you are draining the colored liquid from your body, it may drain slow or fast. Don't rush the process. (**As you exhale, you are draining an amount of negative from your body. Then, as you inhale, you fill the emptied space with white light.**)

NOTE 3: Don't worry if you don't get a color. Just use a color that represents negative to you (like light gray or light brown).

NOTE 4: If you use Stress Buster Breathing every day, stress will have less opportunity to build up in your body.

NOTE 5: The more you change beliefs that aren't working, the less negative will build up in your body.

NOTE 6: After completing the practice, remember to be good to yourself and allow any emotions to come out. Eat healthy food, drink filtered water, and get plenty of rest.

NOTE 7: Be sure to write about any experiences you have over the next two days in your journal!

RELEASING GRIEF, STRESS, ANGER, AND MORE

NOTE 8: <u>**Wait at least 2 days before doing the next practice!**</u> This is to allow time for your body, mind, and spirit to adjust.

Practice: Chakra Clearing with Archangel Metatron

Archangel Metatron is one of two archangels who lived a human life on Earth. He is the keeper of sacred geometry (Tree of Life, Flower of Life). Metatron was known as Enoch when he walked the Earth. Sacred geometry represents everything in the universe. It's the key to how everything works and balances itself.

<u>This practice is designed to help you</u>:
Cleanse, clear, balance, and align all your chakras.

<u>When you can do this practice</u>:
Do this practice anytime you feel over-stressed or experience grief, drama, or trauma. Suggest completing the practice during your relax/wind down period after your workday, but you can do it anytime.

<u>Time needed</u>: 5 minutes.

What you will need:

1. A quiet, comfortable space. (Outdoors preferred.)
2. Something comfortable to lay on.
3. Your journal and something to write with.

Reminder:
Review the entire practice (including the notes) before completing it.

Follow these steps:

1. Lay in a comfortable position (preferably on your back).
2. **Breathe in**. Through your nose, slowly filling your belly with air.
3. **Breathe out**. Through your mouth, slow and easy, until your belly goes flat.
4. **Repeat** 4 cycles of deep breathing.
5. **Ask**: "Archangel Metatron, please cleanse, clear, balance, and align all my chakras using sacred geometry. Thank you."

6. **Breathe in and visualize**: The chakra colors (clear and bright red, yellow, green, blue, purple, white, and any others you are familiar with) in your mind's eye. (Not required, but helpful for focus.)
7. **Breathe out**: Exhale any remaining stress and relax.
8. **Continue cycles** of breathing and imagery until you feel relaxed and finished.

NOTE 1: The first time you do the practice, you may feel sensations like relaxation, waves of energy, zings, prickles, etc. You may see, hear, or feel images, colors, or sensations coming from your chest, stomach, or other areas. You may also see colors or other things and hear sounds. What you experience will be unique to you. Don't worry, there's no cause for alarm as this is normal. Just continue to deep breathe and relax.

NOTE 2: The Chakra Energy Network is an expansive energy center network that extends far beyond the seven major chakras. It comprises 114 chakras (7 major chakras, 21 minor chakras, and 86 micro chakras). It also has 72,000 nadis (36,000 on each side of the body). The nadis are an energy flow linked to the sleep cycle, the circadian rhythm, and the ultradian rhythm of the body.

The nadis connect with the navel, heart, and brain areas of the body. These nadis operate through collaboration and interaction as interconnected energy beings.

NOTE 3: Be sure to write about any experiences you have from this practice in your journal!

Practice: Grief Release

How do we know if we have grief that needs to be released? Do you avoid talking about certain people from the past? Has one or more deaths of loved ones been especially hard to "get over"? Are there certain things that trigger overwhelming emotions (like a song, a photo, a memory)? Is there one person who passed away years ago, yet any reminder of them instantly brings you to tears? If any of these circumstances sound familiar, you may be holding onto grief.

A Yakima grandmother once told me that tears are a gift from Great Spirit (Source). They help us release our grief. Releasing feels good for our body, mind, and spirit. When we keep things inside, we can make ourselves sick.

This practice is designed to help you:
Begin the process of releasing any grief you **may** have stored in your body, mind, or spirit. It will also reduce heart pain from loss.

RELEASING GRIEF, STRESS, ANGER, AND MORE

This practice sets your intent to release in the way that is best for you! You do not have to recall or relive any grief events for this practice to work!

<u>When you can do this practice</u>:
You only have to do this practice once. (If you experience another death or grief event in the future, complete this practice again. It will help you grieve properly at the outset.) This practice **must** be completed outside if at all possible!

<u>Time needed</u>: 10 minutes.

<u>What You Will Need</u>:

1. A quiet space outside where you won't be interrupted for at least 10 minutes.
2. Something comfortable to sit or lay on.
3. <u>Essential Oil</u>: Sweet Marjoram (optional). (<u>Sweet Marjoram</u> reduces levels of stress, anxiety, and grief. It also helps balance the body and mind.)

4. <u>Crystal</u>: Blue Fluorite (optional). (Blue fluorite helps release anything trapped in your mind you cannot seem to let go. It will also assist in releasing disappointments, suppressed feelings, and frustrations. The stone resonates excellently with the throat chakra.)
5. Your journal and something to write with.

<u>Reminder</u>:
Review the entire practice (including the notes) before completing it.

<u>Follow these steps</u>:

1. Sit or lay in a comfortable position on the ground. (Placing your bare feet on the ground will strengthen the effects of this practice.)
2. **Breathe in**. Through your nose, slowly filling your belly with air.
3. **Breathe out and say aloud**: "I am releasing any grief that no longer serves my Highest Good."
4. **Breathe in and say**: "I am."
5. **Apply**: 1 drop of Sweet Marjoram essential oil onto your skin and/or inhale the scent (optional).

6. **Hold**: The blue fluorite crystal in your non-writing hand (optional).
7. **Breathe in**. Through your nose, slowly filling your belly with air.
8. **Breathe out**. Through your mouth, slow and easy until your belly goes flat.
9. **Repeat** 4 cycles of deep breathing.
10. **Say aloud**: "Creator (God, Universe, Source, Spirit, etc.), help me find peace and healing in my heart for my loved ones who have passed from this world. Help me know they are where they need to be and have found rest and peace. I ask for help to carry on in life and recognize all is known, understood, and forgiven. Thank you!"
11. **Continue deep breathing**. Allow any emotions, feelings, thoughts, to come out. Take as long as you need until you feel you are finished. Once you're done, give thanks for the release!

NOTE 1: If you're unable to sit or lay on the ground, use a chair, step stool, wheelchair, or other to sit with the soles of your feet on the ground.

NOTE 2: Focus on your deep breathing. Allow random thoughts, sensations, or feelings to pass.

NOTE 3: Never assume there is grief or negative in your body! Simply allow whatever grief that <u>may</u> be there to be released.

NOTE 4: During this practice you may experience physical sensations and/or strong emotions. Everyone is different. Don't be alarmed. This is normal.

NOTE 5: Don't worry about the practice being too much for you to handle. You'll only experience what you need right now. You are ready!

NOTE 6: Be sure to write about any experiences you have over the next seven days in your journal!

NOTE 7: **<u>Wait at least 7 days before doing any other practices</u>!** This is to allow yourself time to adjust and release. (If you are still releasing grief after seven days, wait an additional seven days before completing any other practices.) When you feel a sense of peace (and your emotions have calmed) you will be ready to move on to the next chapter.

In this chapter, we've learned the importance of giving release to any negative that may be stored in our bodies. We also understand our body and mind work to help us find balance with our new beliefs.

We now have four practices we can use for the rest of our lives (when needed) to relieve stress, restore energy and balance, and release negativity or grief. Make these exercises a regular part of your life to release the negativity that causes stress, worry, or sadness.

Living a spiritual life has many aspects. Each new habit or belief we adopt will improve our overall well-being. Let's examine these aspects and uncover some daily tips and advice.

11
Living a Spiritual Life

*Focus on the positive, good things in life . . .
and feel the joy in it!*

As we've discussed throughout this book, it's important to maintain a balance between our body, mind, and spirit. When we do, we experience a good, healthful life. In the previous chapter, we added to our spiritual toolbox practices to help us maintain that balance. We'll take a mini-tour of some additional tools we can use to live a balanced life in this chapter. We will also reveal some secrets and tips on how to use these tools. Most of us live our daily lives through the comfortable habits we've formed. We stick to our routine during the work week. We wake up, shower, eat, commute, work all day, commute again, eat dinner, watch TV, and then go to bed. This lifestyle is fine if your life is fulfilling and happy.

Reduced stress, better spiritual communication, improved health, and increased energy are just some benefits of the daily spiritual practices listed below.

1. Get great sleep.
2. Analyze your dreams.
3. Think, say, do, and feel positives.
4. Rethink your beliefs.
5. Eat healthy foods and exercise.
6. Drink water.
7. Release/heal the past.
8. Stay healed.
9. Take everything in baby steps.
10. Love and be patient with yourself.
11. Learn and try new stuff.
12. Take your time.

Let's examine each of these daily practices . . .

Get great sleep.

Our body, mind, and spirit need at least six to eight hours of sleep each night. This gives us time to rest and rejuvenate. Our mind needs time to sort, review, and file all we experienced during our day.

Source needs an opportunity to communicate with us while our mind is at rest and our body relaxed. The benefits are more energy, a clearer mind, and receiving much needed guidance!

We may believe our day starts when we wake up, but the truth is . . . it begins <u>before</u> we go to sleep! Whatever we are giving our energy and attention to as we get ready for sleep is what the subconscious works on for eight hours to bring into our lives! Ensuring our thoughts, words, actions, and emotions are positive before sleep is one of the most important things we can do to improve our lives.

Here are a few sleep tips:

1. Never go to sleep angry or upset! Instead, do your Reinforcing Before Sleep Sequence (from Chapter 9, Exercise 6).
2. Start preparing for sleep at least one hour before bedtime. This means not using any electronic devices (phone, TV, computer, games, etc.). Some things you can do instead are:
    - Take a warm shower.
    - Listen to relaxing music.
    - Read a positive book.
    - Do deep breathing exercises.
    - Stretch your muscles.
    - Write in your journal using positive language.

- Whatever relaxes you!
3. Remove ALL electronics from your sleep space. This includes TVs, cellphones, computers, smartwatches, Wi-Fi routers, or any other "smart" device. Your bedroom is for sleep. Electronics will interrupt your sleep cycle!
4. Turn off your Wi-Fi at night. The signal interferes with your sleep!
5. Make sure your sleep space is comfortable.

Analyze your dreams.

Many people say they don't dream or can't remember their dreams. If you believe you don't have dreams (or can't remember them), you should have these on your list of beliefs to change. We all dream as dreams are a part of our Source OS and a tool for sending us helpful communication. Perhaps we believe we don't dream because we haven't been able to remember our dreams. Sometimes, we don't remember our dreams because we don't sleep well. Beliefs, sleeping well, and dreams are all interrelated.

The best way to remember dreams is to <u>believe</u> you can remember your dreams! Here are some tips:

1. Set your intent to remember your dreams by buying a small notebook and placing it (and a pen) next to your bed. (Write, "My Dream Journal" on the front cover.)
2. Before getting into bed, touch your dream journal and say, "I am remembering my dreams".
3. Write down your dream as soon as you wake from it (even if it's the middle of the night). Write down everything you can remember (people, places, things, numbers, colors, etc.). If you don't write down your dream as soon as you wake from it, you may forget it by morning.
4. Once you've written down your dream, come back later to figure out what it means. (I like to analyze my dreams each morning.) To understand a dream, just think about what it means to you. Spiritual communication will always be in your language and from your point of view.

For example: What thoughts or emotions do you experience when you think of snakes? The time on a clock? The ocean? A mansion? The answer will be based on your own personal experiences and beliefs.

NOTE 1: You can buy a dream dictionary if you want, but it's not necessary. You are your own walking dream dictionary!

NOTE 2: It may take a few days for you to remember your dreams, so don't get discouraged.

NOTE 3: Using your unique perspective (for dreams and more) will be extensively covered in a future book in this series. Until then, here's a tip for translating spiritual messages:

> Spiritual information you receive is customized to your inherent and learned knowledge. (It speaks your language.) This helps you understand it. If you have any difficulty understanding what you are receiving, ask, "What does this mean to me?"

Think, say, do, and feel positives.

We covered this in chapters five and six. Words, thoughts, actions, and emotions have the power to create or destroy. What we focus on the most creates our reality in life. Develop a habit of choosing positive thoughts, words, actions, and feelings before you release them into the world.

This concept cannot be stressed enough. You create the positive or negative you experience in life in real-time! If you want a happier, more positive life, you must create it throughout your day by changing the thoughts, words, actions, and feelings you are using. A magic pill that can do it for you does not exist. The magic is inside you in the form of what you choose to think, say, do, and feel!

Rethink your beliefs.

Be open to discovering truths you may be unaware of. Be willing to change any belief that doesn't have a positive influence on your life. (Refer to chapters seven through nine and complete the exercises again at any time.)

Your current life experience is a direct result of your beliefs. As children, we didn't have a choice of what to believe. Once we're adults, the sole responsibility for our beliefs is on us. Earlier, we discussed a need to change beliefs if you're only operating from your learned knowledge and you aren't experiencing a happy life.

Eat healthy foods and exercise.

Information on eating healthy and exercise could fill many books. The tip I'll share (for now) about food is <u>clean and local</u>. We are what we eat and drink! (The higher the quality of your food and drink, the less you'll need medications now and in the future.) Choose local, farm-raised, organic, pesticide-free, growth hormone-free meats, veggies, cheeses, etc. Ditch the fast-food and processed foods! Learn how to read labels!

Exercise doesn't have to be running a marathon or lifting weights five times a week (unless that's what you want to do). Walking for twenty minutes, three or four times a week, will improve circulation, help you drop a few pounds, gain some muscle mass, relax you, and give you more energy! Even if you can't walk, run, or lift weights, get outside and get some fresh air and sunshine! Twenty minutes will improve your mood and give you some of the Vitamin D your body needs.

NOTE 1: Always consult your primary care physician or mental health professional before changing your diet or exercise program.

NOTE 2: A great resource for eating healthy and healing a variety of chronic illnesses through food is *The Healing Revolution Diet* by Dr. Randall S. Hansen, Ph.D. Check it out here: **https://amzn.to/3U6Yo9A**

Drink water.

Our bodies contain a lot of water. Water acts like the body's antifreeze by helping regulate our temperature. The more hydrated we are, the better we can handle prolonged exposure to heat or cold. Water also helps flush out any toxins we may have in our bodies.

Drink spring, reverse osmosis (RO), purified, or distilled water. (The RO and distillation processes may remove essential minerals. Use a dash of high quality mineral salt in your water to add any minerals you may need.)

No tap water (unless it's fluoride-free and filtered)! Tap water contains chlorine, fluoride (depending on where you live), heavy metals, and other chemicals (depending on its source). Bottled water labeled "Drinking Water" is tap water (from a municipal water source) put in a bottle! Always check the label for the source. You can purchase a filtered water pitcher to filter tap water, or a filtered portable water bottle. Recommend buying flats of bottled spring, RO, purified, or distilled water to keep in case of emergency.

Release/heal the past.

Decide you will not carry around negativity from the past anymore. Use the exercises in Chapter Ten to assist you. If past people or experiences do come up, ask what you need to learn, give thanks for the lesson, and then let it go! Past hurts, grief, trauma, and drama aspire to be released! Allow them to be on their way.

Don't hold grudges or seek revenge. It will only hurt you because you're carrying around the negative and not releasing it. The longer negative stays inside us, the more it will manifest itself as a physical or mental disease! Remember, what we send out comes back to us, so we need to make sure it's all good!

Stay healed.

Once you've released the past, and changed your beliefs and habits, don't go back to what you were doing before! We have the power to create a better life, but we can't allow old beliefs to creep back into our lives. If we do, the old results will return. Much like a person who goes on a diet and loses twenty pounds, then returns to their old eating habits. They will gain back the pounds they lost, and more!

Go back and review the first seven chapters anytime. Practice holding the spiritual truths in your body.

Repeat the healing exercises from Chapter Ten. Be patient and good to yourself!

Take everything in baby steps.

Whatever changes you want to make, take baby steps to get there. Baby steps are changing one or two things at a time versus trying to change them all at once. There's no rush! You're not in some spiritual race. Besides, all things come in your time, when you're ready. Enjoy the process and savor the positive emotions and results that come from your efforts. If you pick one thing and stick with it, you won't have to worry about being overwhelmed.

You may have heard the saying, "God does not give us more than we can handle" (or similar). Have faith that you ARE strong enough, smart enough, and worthy enough to change your life.

Love and be patient with yourself.

We often love and give to others, but struggle to love ourselves. To love others, we must love ourselves. We cannot give to others what we do not have ourselves. So, give yourself a break. Don't push yourself to burnout.

Set aside a few moments every day to unwind and find inner peace. Practice patience. Know you are making progress every time you reinforce your new beliefs. Watch how your life improves with your new beliefs and practices! Celebrate as you become more positive and happy!

Visualizing a new belief manifesting in your life is powerful! Don't wait for it to happen. Live life as if it has already happened. That's why it's SO important to experience what it feels like to have your new belief. Don't allow your five senses to tarnish the vision and positivity you have about your life with your new belief.

Learn and try new stuff.

1. Make your living spaces warm and inviting. (Declutter and clean your home. Make sure you have breathing room . . . you don't have to fill every corner and open space.)
2. Discover and practice (experience) your spiritual gifts. (Take a class on a spiritual topic that includes actual practices so you can EXPERIENCE it.)
3. Create your spiritual practices and use them daily. (Schedule when you will do your meditation, relax time, belief work, or other. Stick to your schedule!)

4. Recognize and use the spiritual help around you. (Pay attention to any out of the ordinary experiences you have. Write about them in your journal. Figure out what they mean.)

Take your time.

As mentioned earlier, we must experience our spiritual lessons for them to be learned and remembered. Everyone experiences at their own pace, so don't rush the process or think it's some kind of competition. Here are some helpful tips:

1. Once you master a skill or practice, then you can tailor it to you. (Source can show you "your way" to do it.)
2. Spirit (Universe, God, Gaia, etc.) will communicate with you in ways you understand. (Source won't tell you what to do, but will give you advice and suggestions. The communication may be direct, stern, funny, etc.)
3. When you use methods that are natural/comfortable for you, it will be easier to practice them on a regular basis.

4. Notice what you're attracted to, what's going on around you, and what you're feeling inside. Certain situations or people will continue to show up in your life as a reminder that there's something you need to fix, learn, or let go of. Remember, coincidences do not exist.

In this chapter, we covered some tips and tools to further assist you in living a spiritual life. We revealed the big secret of when our day starts. The results you'll experience using these tips and advice increase in power if you incorporate them into your daily life. Don't wait to start taking action! The sooner you start, the quicker you'll experience less stress, more energy, and more!

Integrate the practices from this chapter into your life, one by one. Pick one practice from the list and take action now (like drinking good, clean water). Once you've incorporated one into your daily routine, select another one to add to your life.

12
Conclusion

*Once our eyes are opened
we can no longer go back to sleep.*

By discovering the truth about spiritual gifts, we wake our own from their slumber. These spiritual abilities are an extension of our five senses, but we use them in a spiritual way versus a physical. We all have all the spiritual gifts, but how we use them varies from person to person. One or two of these abilities will be stronger when we first start using them. The more we use the strong ones, the stronger the weaker ones become. How we choose to use them (or IF we choose to use them) is up to each individual (Free Will).

We've learned our Source OS (inherent knowledge) plays a crucial role in maintaining life balance. Without it, we experience disharmony in our lives as stress, recurring drama, trauma, and other negative experiences.

We also learned (for most of us) that our spiritual gifts were not part of our childhood training. Our teachers instilled in us the reliance on our learned knowledge to navigate through life.

So, we have lived our lives doing the best we know how, with a critical piece of knowledge missing. Thinking, saying, doing, and feeling the way we witnessed (and accepted as truth) as children. Believing this was the way we should live our lives as well. We didn't learn (until now) that everything we focus our energy and attention on is what our subconscious mind works on bringing into our lives. Now we understand how we can use this creative power to bring balance and positivity back into our human experience.

We were unaware of many spiritual truths because we didn't even know we had a built-in, inherent knowledge package (Source OS). As we experienced these spiritual truths, we realized the depth of their opposition to many of the things we were told by others or taught to believe when we were children. Now we know the truth and can release any falsehood from the past (if we choose to do so).

We explored our beliefs about ourselves, others, and the world. In doing so, we came to know which of our beliefs were causing an imbalance in our lives and not aligned with spiritual truth.

CONCLUSION

Choosing the first belief we wanted to change seemed like a daunting task, but the practice we used made getting started a lot easier. Now we are feeling and seeing the results of our old belief release.

Using the healing practices helped us feel more energized and grounded. We let go of some (or all) of the stress, negative, drama, trauma, or grief we'd been carrying around with us for a long time. As we master these practices, we can make them a part of our life. Anytime we sense the need for release, grounding, energizing, or balance, we can use them. We can also make the spiritual lifestyle tips a part of our daily routine.

We should remember the best way to tell if we have beliefs we need to change is by looking at our daily life experience. When we're happy (and the many aspects of our lives are in balance), our beliefs are serving us well. Our life aspects (or life areas) are our careers, finances, spiritual practices, health, sexuality, and relationships. One of my former mentors wrote: "If your life sucks, it's not the life you were meant to live. Change it." (Excerpt from *Radical Rebirth* by Randy Gage.)

We change our life by changing the hand-me-down beliefs we accepted as true that are making our lives a hot mess. We change our life by breaking old habits that keep us in a cycle of negative results. Being open to rethinking what we believe about ourselves (and our spiritual gifts) is a successful first step in our spiritual journey.

If you're still having doubts about your spiritual abilities . . . make sure you complete the exercises and intentions in this book. Pay attention to experiences you have, messages you get, coincidences that cross your path, and dreams you have for the next 30 days. Write about them in your journal. When you get a message (feel or hear something, see something, know something, get a warning or gut feeling, etc.), write them down and say, "Thank you."

In reading this book over the last few weeks, you've given yourself the gift of rediscovering the Spirit that lives within. The Spirit Within has always been there. It has been waiting for the right time for you to wake it. Now you are free to realize the potential of the power of creation you carry inside you. A celebration is in order! You have experienced your first spiritual journey! May it be the first of many to come.

Please Leave a Review!

Reviews really help independent authors like me! If you enjoyed *Walking the Path*, please leave a review at your favorite bookstore:

books2read.com/walking-the-path

BONUS: Staying Calm in a World Gone Slightly Mad
(A Q&A Guide)

Q: What is the easiest thing I can do to make the greatest positive impact on my life?

A: Recognize and avoid activities (or people) that are consistently negative.

How do we know if they are negative? If engaging with them causes negative emotions, drains your energy, or creates drama.

Some sources of negative may be social media, watching the news, certain TV programs, movies, books, or any other outlet that is negative. We should limit our time or avoid interacting with negative sources.

Focus on the positive (abundance, blessings, close family and friends, special moments, joyful news, etc.).

Q: What can I do to change all the negative that bombards me every day?

A: Stop allowing it to overwhelm you or negatively affect your day.

We all have Free Will. We decide if we <u>allow</u> something (or someone) to make us (or keep us) angry, upset, afraid, stressed, or depressed.

1. Don't watch/listen/read any fear, hate, or division type materials. (Mainstream news, certain content creators on social media platforms, certain politicians or other "influencers".) Don't give them your energy or attention.
2. Stop waiting for someone/something to come along and save you, your community, or your nation! Save yourself. Help others. Spread positive, truth, hope, and caring. DO things to assist others.
3. Let go of any fear, anger, hate, or anxiety you may be experiencing. CHOOSE to be happy, helpful, loving, caring, etc. We increase the power of negative when we put out negative! It's its power source! In other words, negative feeds off of negative. It's how negative keeps its power!
4. Start <u>being</u> the change you wish to see in the world.

Giving away our power and responsibility, remaining silent, our want of instant gratification, consumerism, and not keeping politicians (and others) in "check" is what helped breed our current situation. Doing the opposite will help speed up change for the better.

Q: What can I do to make a positive difference in my community?

A: DO things to help others in your community (volunteer).

There are many ways to help! Volunteer at a food pantry, pet shelter, elder home, after-school program, serve on a council, attend meetings with community leaders, or distribute goods to the homeless . . . just to name a few. Everyone has skills and abilities! Use yours or learn some new ones.

Spread the positive and the "WE" versus the negative and division. Think, say, do, and feel positives.

Q: What can I do to make a positive difference in the world?

A: Be a decent human being.

Do not leave your fellow humans out to dry. What comes for them (like disasters, oppression, or poverty) <u>WILL</u> come for you. History has proven this over and over again.

Send love (or prayers) to those responsible for evil/destructive acts. Love is stronger than ANY negative!

Defend yourself when necessary (if you don't know how, learn). Speak up versus remaining silent (silence is consent).

Q: How can one person fix all that is wrong in the world?

A: One person can be an inspiration to others with the positive example they set. Positivity is like negativity in that it's contagious. It spreads like a ripple upon the water after a stone breaks the surface.

The operative word here is WE. It's not me, us, or them . . . but WE. This is why some people sow the seeds of division. They know how powerful the people are when they are united. WE must recognize and use our power to overcome all the negative. If we want the time of positive changes to arrive more quickly, we must end the negative and division!

Love is stronger than any negative power. WE neutralize negative with positive (love).

Q: How can I send love to horrible people who do bad things?

A: You can imagine surrounding them with white or pink light and saying aloud, "I am sending this person love". (This is especially important to example to children. Teach them how to live/send out positive!)

If you aren't able to send them love, then ask for a blessing. Say aloud, "I ask that this person be sent a blessing that is for their Highest Good and in full alignment with their Divine Self. Thank you."

If you watch a video, read a tweet, view a TikTok, or whatever that's negative, send the originator the blessing above and stop watching/reading the content. Spend your valuable time on something positive!

Q: What can I do about all the negative on my social media feeds?

A: Decide that you will no longer spend your time, energy, or attention on the negative.

One of the reasons there are so many negative content creators is because people watch their content! They are making money by spreading negativity. So, let them know by not watching, unsubscribing, leaving a polite comment telling them why you're unsubscribing, giving a thumbs down or whatever, so they get the hint. If people stop watching, they'll change what they're doing or go away.

REMINDER: You choose how you want to create/live your life. Change comes when we choose love. When we decide to not allow others to manipulate our emotions on the daily. When we practice and trust our inherent gifts and abilities.

Q: How can I tell if my words, thoughts, actions, and emotions are having a negative effect on my life and the world at large?

A: Think back over the last few years (since your last election, since the pandemic started, or any major events in your country). During these time periods or events, how much time did you spend on negative thoughts, words, or actions? How many days were you afraid, worried, stressed, anxious, or depressed?

Now, think about what you're experiencing in your daily life now.

How many hours of the day are you afraid, angry, sad, or stressed out? What is your country like now? Do you see things getting better or worse? If your life (and the place you live) is more negative than positive, it's a clue that more positive and love are needed.

We all have Free Will. We can choose to do whatever we want. But what you send out comes back to you! It comes back in the form of your daily life experiences. It all starts with you! What this means is, the more people send out positive, the more positive there will be in the world.

Q: What is the most powerful, positive thing I can do each day to improve my life?

A1: Think, say, do, and feel positives throughout your day.

What we send out comes back to us! Be careful of the type of thoughts, words, feelings, and actions you are sending out into the world.

Thoughts, words, feelings, and actions have power . . . they create what we are experiencing in our daily lives.

All we have to do to change the quality of our daily experience is to change our think, say, do, and feel! If we want positive in our world, we must think, say, do, and feel positives throughout our day!

A2: Focus on what you want to experience in life before you go to sleep.

What we focus on before we go to sleep at night is what we create for the days to come. Occupy your mind and body with positives as you wind down from your day. (Listen to relaxing music, take a warm bath, read an uplifting book, etc.)

After you get in bed, take slow, deep breaths to relax. Visualize the life you want to live, how good it feels, and how good you feel living it. Imagine the world at peace and beautiful. See yourself as happy, content, and loved! Do the deep breathing and visualizations until you fall asleep.

I hope you found this bonus section useful for assisting you in navigating our ever-challenging world.

Blessings to you!
De

When is the Last Time You Had a Great Night's Sleep?

Does it take you forever to fall asleep or you have trouble staying asleep?

Do you struggle with restlessness, frequent bathroom trips, or constant fatigue?

If this sounds like your "normal" nights sleep . . . and you're ready to get the quality of sleep you truly deserve . . . sign up to get your copy of *Get Your Best Sleep Ever!* here: **subscribepage.io/Sleep**

This sleep guide will help you:

1. Increase energy, reduce stress, and enhance clarity of thought.
2. Get more hours of quality sleep.
3. Reduce or eliminate all those trips to the bathroom.
4. Stop the tossing and turning all night.
5. Fall asleep faster and stay asleep longer.

(When you sign up, you'll also receive tips, discounts, insider firsts, and be notified when I release a new book!)

If you've had enough days of being tired, sleepy, cranky, and mentally exhausted, get your sleep guide and start transforming your sleep today!

Get Your Best Sleep Ever! provides 3 simple ways to ensure you get better sleep . . .

- Revamp your sleeping space for ultimate sleepability.
- Things you can do during the day to set yourself up for great sleep at night.
- Creating a bedtime ritual that gets you sleeping fast!

And getting your best sleep ever doesn't have to cost you a thing!

So, if you're ready to get the great sleep you've been wanting, just go here: **subscribepage.io/Sleep** to get your complimentary copy of *Get Your Best Sleep Ever!*

May your future sleep be peaceful and restful!
De

About the Author

De is best known for her ability to explain complex spiritual concepts through simple tips and practices. She believes that spirituality is supposed to be simple!

She has had spiritual experiences since she was a child. The real-life stories, spiritual knowledge, and experiences she shares come from her twenty-plus-year professional and spiritual journey.

Her education includes a Master of Education Degree. She enjoys writing, public speaking, teaching, and coaching. She has the unique ability to bring realism and humor into her creations.

De is an author and speaker of living a simple, spirit-full life.

Learn more about De at: **DeFletcher.com**.
There you will find links to all her social media, freebies, and new books!

FOLLOW DE FLETCHER

Website:
DeFletcher.com

BookBub:
bookbub.com/authors/de-fletcher
Be the first to know when I have a new release, preorder, or discount!

Books 2 Read:
Books2read.com/DeFletcher
Click the "Follow This Author" button to see my *Reading List* and get notified when I publish my next book!

Amazon:
Amazon.com/author/defletcher
Click the "Follow" button to get updates on new releases!

COMING SOON!

Can't wait to read Book 2 in the *Simple Spiritual Journey* series?

Healing Practices for the Body, Mind, & Spirit

Sick of feeling tired, afraid, stressed, or angry in the constantly changing world we live in?

If you're ready to take back your energy and zest for life, and stay balanced no matter what the world may throw at you . . . this book is a must-have!

Discover simple practices and tips that help you:
- Reduce stress, worry, and frustration
- Increase your energy level and stamina
- Release negative, anger, and grief
- Get better sleep
- Maintain balance in your life

Be the first to know when Book 2 is released!
Go to: **DeFletcher.com** and sign up on the home page!

(You'll also receive spiritual tips, discounts, cover reveals, and more!)

Are you a fan of the strange, dark, and mysterious?

If you like a good creep-out every now and then, this book won't disappoint!

True Stories of the Strange & Unusual

From bizarre to funny . . .
Heart-wrenching to hair-raising . . .
And most things in-between.

An inside look into the strange life of a psychic medium! A wild ride filled with real-life stories of the paranormal!

Sign up at: **subscribepage.io/Sleep** and be the first to know when these books get released! (You'll also get a copy of *Get Your Best Sleep Ever!* and exclusive perks and discounts.)

Check out all of De's books here:
defletcher.com/pages/spiritual-books

Also by De Fletcher

Born a Poor, Black, Indian, White Girl (A Memoir) is a real page-turner about an intense journey through identity crisis, abuse, poverty, racism, and grief.

De shares her personal stories in an open and honest way, as if she were talking with a close friend. Her journey is heart-wrenching, funny, emotional, and inspirational!

"Born" is an origin story that shares hard-learned lessons about life and overcoming childhood trauma.

Pick up a copy today!
At Amazon: **Amazon.com/dp/B07BVJD84Q**

OR

From your favorite bookstore:
Books2Read.com/Born

Not ready to buy?
Check out an excerpt from the book here:
bktry.com/vDRmQSxc

Acknowledgements

A special thank-you to all the members of my review and launch teams. You guys are simply awesome!

A warm and sincere thanks to all my friends and family who continue to support my Indie Author career.

Thank you Francis at *100 Covers* for the cover design!

www.ingramcontent.com/pod-product-compliance
Lightning Source LLC
Chambersburg PA
CBHW052138070526
44585CB00017B/1876